I0187878

THE TOP 100 DREAM IGNITER

Copyright © 2021 by Grant R. Nieddu, State of the Spark LLC

All rights reserved. No part of this publication may be reproduced, distributed, or transmitted in any form or by any means, including photocopying, recording, or other electronic or mechanical methods, without the prior written permission of the publisher, except in the case of brief quotations embodied in critical reviews and certain other noncommercial uses permitted by copyright law. For permission requests, write to the author, addressed "Attention: Permissions " at Grant@StateoftheSpark.com

Grant R. Nieddu
State of the Spark LLC
P O Box 2115
Lakeland, FL 33806
www.StateoftheSpark.com

Ordering Information:
For details, contact Grant@StateoftheSpark.com.

Print ISBN: 978-0-578-85984-2

Printed in the United States of America on SFI Certified paper.

Fourth Edition

THE TOP 100 DREAM IGNITER

THE STATE OF THE SPARK GOAL-SETTING GUIDE TO IGNITING YOUR LIFE OF EXPLOSIVE SIGNIFICANCE

GRANT R. NIEDDU

CONTENTS

Thank You, Spark Citizen   1

GETTING STARTED RIGHT   *3*
Welcome   5
Drowning Without Dreams   7
Things You Must Know About The Dream Igniter   15

THE SYSTEM   *21*
The Dream-Igniter System   23
Introduction   25
Phase 1: Top 100 List   31
Phase 2: Categorize   45
Phase 3: Easy as A-B-C   53
Phase 4: 1-Year Goals   67
Phase 5: Get S.M.A.R.T.!   97
Phase 6: An Environment for Success   107
Phase 7: Free Gift   123

NEXT STEPS   *125*
So, What Now?   127
Additional Tools for Your Sparked Journey   129
About the Author   133

THANK YOU, SPARK CITIZEN

ALL IT TAKES IS A LITTLE SPARK

You are what drives me.

Everything I do is to empower and equip you, the believer in bigger things, to achieve all that is in your heart.

"Igniting Lives of Explosive Significance"

This has been my mission for years now. Your initiative, in starting this workbook, to take massive action on your goals and dreams, inspires me.

I invite you to take all the time you need with this guide, *The Top 100 Dream Igniter*. I guarantee that if you do each step in this guide, you will achieve radically more than you could have on your own. As you will discover, critical secrets can set the course of your life from stuck to sparked to making an impact in the world.

You are a champion. Thank you again. I look forward to this awesome time together.

Most Gratefully,
Grant R. Nieddu
Founder & Chief Spark Instigator

GETTING STARTED RIGHT

WELCOME

Thank you for taking your life and goals seriously. If you have come this far, you are certainly committed to achieving more than just the dreams on your heart. I know that you are also destined to make a massive impact for good.

The legacy you will leave will be felt by many, and hopefully you will begin to see yourself as you really are: a blessed, radiating individual capable of great things for yourself and others.

I am so excited to be on this journey with you! Before you go any further, I want you to do me two huge favors.

GET COMFORTABLE

I personally love using my Kindle or Google Books to read books.

But, this is not a book. This is a guide.

There are activities to do. You can do them digitally, of course. I encourage you to attempt to do this off line, though. Primarily because writing goals physically helps give birth to them in the physical world.

So, get comfortable and dive in!

TELL US YOU STARTED!

Go to the Spark Goals and Gratitude Facebook group, and tell us you started!

In the comments, tell me you started this document! I love to hear when someone starts on this journey! Let me and the rest of the Spark community know that you have begun.

Here: https://facebook.com/groups/stateofthespark.

START SPARKING: *no one achieves anything in a silo. Success is a team support. Head over to the Facebook Goals and Gratitude group, introduce yourself. You'll feel good once you do.*

Not only is this a great community of Sparked Citizens. There are courses, free resources, and private training materials. Get help from other Spark Citizens like yourself.

This group is the beginning of the Spark mission to bring you the tools, training, and team you need to launch into even bigger things!

Thank you so much, and let's get sparking!

DROWNING WITHOUT DREAMS

The gigantic wave heaved the ship, shuddered the ship from bow to stern, and vibrated my shin bones. I grasped the rail of the stairs to brace. The ship heaved high. The relentless, icy ocean, with the ferocity of leviathan, was powerful to wield a ship this large so easily.

I knew that beneath my feet, below the now-soaked carpet, there was just a few feet of riveted steel, and that, for the next few seconds, was 40 feet of open air between us and black, icy ocean.

The ship's bow pitched forward.

My stomach dropped as I braced for impact. A student's cabin door flew open in the aerial descent. Suspended for a gravity-free moment I saw the port-hole in her room and watched dizzily as the horizon showed endless waves as 50-foot, white, foamy tombstones bearing down on me.

SHUDDERING STEEL SMACKED
HARD UPON IMPACT

I saw the view through the port-hole plunge first into foamy green then disappear into deep pitch black. The cabin door slammed shut. The other students around me regained their footing.

Following the instructions shouted from the intercom, we rallied and returned to our rapid ascent. We were on Deck 2, the lowest deck. In calmer waters, our port-hole windows were submerged in dark blue water. The rest of the students had made it to Deck 5, the deck with the life rafts. We had 3 more floors to climb to the open air.

Insanely, I grinned.

I had set this very trip with Semester-at-Sea in my sights 5 years before wrecking at sea. Reading about the life of adventure and academics when I was 18, I had cut out the advertisement and taped it to the wall. In that moment, years before, it seemed like a dream worth dreaming. That was my first crude vision board and it took me around the world.

At the time, I was not interested in missions (as my wife and I have done), or building businesses around the globe (as we have with the Spark team), or investing in real estate to fund the Spark Mission. I was not interested in ministry (though it would invade my heart in just a few years). I was not interested in helping others accomplish their goals (as I am now with my business, State of the Spark).

When I was 18 nothing interested me more than having fun, living adventures, and surfing epic waves. Jump forward several frustrating years of losing myself in acting and modeling, getting knocked down, being ambushed by the ministry, and then recovering those lost years with that ad taped to my vision board, and you would have found me on that ship.

On the reeling deck of a sinking ship, I was living the very dream I had so many years before. Somehow, through my aimless life, that picture of Semester-at-Sea stuck with me and became real.

And the smack reality of that dream was hitting me in the form of another rolling, icy wave that blew out a window on the ship's bridge, destroying the electronics. The next few hours were a blur of danger as well as heroics by the ship's crew.

Needless to say, we made it. Once we were in the calm of the storm, I collapsed on the marble tile floor. Most had crawled back to their cabins. I just lay there in the middle of the foyer on Deck 5.

I WAS IN SHOCK - I WAS PARALYZED WITH A GALE FORCE IN MY HEART

Much of it was adrenaline and fear. But as these chemicals faded, a peaceful excitement arose in my heart. I probably should have been dwelling more on the fate we had avoided, but I wasn't. I was transfixed on the idea that a cut-out piece of paper had gotten me to this moment of adventure (and peril, yes, that, too).

I had a glimmer that there was something powerful hidden in this experience. The idea that having a visual representation of the desires in my heart actually contributed to the accomplishment of those desires blew my mind. It was a wild theory, and I had no facts to go on; just a hunch.

This idea became hidden as I was swept up in the sense of adventure and excitement I enjoyed on that spring 2005 trip-of-a-lifetime called Semester-at-Sea. It was more than an academic adventure.

It was a passage to what has, so far, been a passionate life of missions, business building, travel, love, and excitement. It carried me around the world, and when I returned I would never be the same.

Upon returning, the idea of writing down and capturing goals visually arrived again. My mentor and friend, Terry Kruse, handed me a unique book, unknown to many (but read by the wealthy), that discussed the principles of goals I discovered during my sea-born revelation.

At the same time we discovered the teachings of another individual who spoke directly about the power of written goals. I am forever grateful for this teacher's work and the commitment he made to help others accomplish their goals.

I HAVE BEEN IN AWE AT THE ADVENTURE MY LIFE HAS BEEN

From then until now, many years later, I have lived in awe. It has not been without serious ups and downs. But I have been in amazement at the adventure my life has been. Somewhere between *creating* my own reality and *discovering* my Divine destiny has been a life of wonder.

Sometimes I think I am making these things happen. Other times I feel like I am on a trip of discovery that would happen with or without my involvement. Whatever it is, written goal-setting is a critical factor to the adventure of my life.

I suspect it will be a critical factor to your life of fulfilment and adventure, too!

If the idea of written goal-setting was not totally embedded in me yet, it was certainly cemented into my being with one particular occurrence in my late 20's that I have to share with you.

On the eve of my 29th birthday I committed that by the same time the following year, on my 30th birthday, that I wanted to have absolute clarity, passion, and peace about my direction in life. Because, at that moment, I had lost everything. Again.

You see, one of my divine adventures led me to getting the job of a lifetime. I was literally paid to read books and deliver talks to a small community of friends. For several years I would show up, read books, learn and grow, and turn that learning into valuable education and tools for this community to grow and impact their city.

During this time my work on the mission field in Haiti with Kenny Ellis bloomed. We founded CPI Haiti, made numerous trips to help, and even had the honor of helping to complete the Chauffard Community Center. (I even wrote a book about it, *'HOPE from Here to Haiti'*). You can check it out here:

https://www.amazon.com/H-P-Here-Haiti-ebook/dp/B009FA9FX4

I met an amazing group of like-minded, intellectual friends. I was in charge of my time. I was free to travel, flying from California to Haiti dozens of times a year.

However, on a particular return trip from Haiti, we were informed that our funding was cut. I was out of work. I had no clients. I had no income (I had not thought about getting a job in years!) Since my employers had given us the house we lived in (which was well beyond our pay), we suddenly had nowhere to live!

The economy in 2008 had sunk. Along with my employers' funding, many jobs were being cut, and job opportunities for "Book Reader" were slim. Finally, after 3 hard months of job searching I had found work; I began selling greeting cards in a greeting card store making minimum wage.

FROM GREATNESS TO GREETING CARDS

Talk about humbling!

On the way to this minimum wage job one day I had hit the brick wall of life. Things were crappy. I was totally depressed. Divine intervention, adventure, or any help at all, felt a million miles away. To make matters worse, with all the life experiences and mental tools I had acquired, I still only had enough money for a single cup of coffee that day. I pulled into the Starbucks across the street, bought a cup of coffee and pulled out my journal (which was just a yellow note pad, the only thing I could afford).

My heart was a rotting hulk of a ship embedded on the ocean floor.

Though I had the encouragement of loving friends and family, their ability to help my financial situation was non-existent. My pride was hurt. I was supposed to be this well-read teacher and trainer.

And at that point I was also *dead broke*.

Grayness set into my vision. Since my trip with Semester-at-Sea, whenever I experienced bouts of depression I was swept out in the angry tide of the gray and bleakness of that storm I experienced in the North Pacific. It felt like all of the chilling waves and sea-sickness was rolling in my stomach in that coffee shop.

I had managed million-dollar properties.
I had founded a non-profit in Haiti.

I had traveled the world, written and published,
and spoken to audiences of all sizes.

I have since built successful companies, partnered
with powerful fortune 500 companies, and built
websites for billion-dollar companies.

But, this time, while swimming in my coffee before my pride-drowning work of selling greeting cards, I caught a spark. This spark somehow began to stir in me.

I thought of all the things I had seen and experienced, all of the danger and risk I had been spared. And I glanced over a few of my written goals.

Suddenly, from sparked to excited, I pondered the power of written goals. I considered the electric power of words and pictures on paper, and their ability to ignite the neurochemicals and power in men and women. All the teachings of my early twenties came rushing into my spirit like an explosive confidence, pushing away the grey tide in my heart and making way to warmer, beautiful waters.

How did millionaires lose everything and start again? How did Nelson Mandela spend so long in prison and come out to change a nation, then the world? How did Jesus' teachings change the world so deeply? And ancient prophets, how had they done it?

These ideas, solutions, and words of ancient wisdom boiled over inside of me. My skin was jumping. My stomach was excited. Compared to the depression I had when I walked into that coffee shop, it was like getting smacked with an electrically charged baseball bat.

> *"Write the vision and make it plain*
> *that he who reads it may run with it."*
> – The Prophet Habakkuk 700 BC

I leapt up from my chair, pen in hand, staring down at that blank sheet of paper.

Words raced before my eyes. They were the words of the things I still wanted to do, see, and be. I saw myself still working on the mission field. I saw myself still helping people accomplish their dreams and visions. I saw myself living a life as an example to my friends and family back home. I saw fitness and health. I saw my relationships with family repaired. I saw resources in the bank. I saw a happy marriage.

And I wept to myself. I wept quietly staring at that blank sheet of paper.

"You ok?" the baristas asked me unexpectedly.

"Yes," I said, now loud with confidence. The lady in the back startled up from her chair and glanced my way. Louder still, I said, *"Yes I am."*

I sat back down and wrote.

I wrote what I saw in my heart. I began writing and penning out every-thing I saw like an electric current from my heart through my mind, my hand. I unabashedly confessed my desires and yearnings to that sheet of paper, that palette of dreams. Each sentence was a sparking flash of lightning back from my mind to my heart, affirming that those ideas and desires were good and would come to pass.

> **START SPARKING:** *Right now, pause, and jot down on any scrap of paper something you crave for yourself but have been putting off. You will feel exhilarated once you do! The rest of this document should make you feel like this and more! I crave:*

_____

_____

_____

_____

_____

And as I said before, I determined by the same time the next year when I was turning 30 that I wanted to have absolute clarity, passion, and peace about my direction in life.

I put the pen down and audibly exhaled. Still excited, I stood and turned from the plate glass windows to the employees of the coffee shop. Without restraint I told those baristas about the power of goal-setting and having direction. They just smiled and nodded at me, the crazy guy on the way to his job at the card store.

But the things I wrote are exactly what happened for me. Despite starting that very day distracted with life, having lost all of my income, finding myself without a home, job, or money, and starting at square one; by the time I turned 30 I had the clarity, passion, and peace I sought.

In fact, **by that same time the next year, I was the boss at that store and managing those very same baristas.**

More than mere clarity, passion, and peace (which are pretty good in themselves), in just a year I had found myself managing at that Fortune 500 company, driving a debt-free new car, working half of my time in Haiti, experiencing an adventurous and passionate relationship with the woman who has since become my wife, and living a life of abundance like I have never known.

Two years later, I was living part-time on this gorgeous island of Hispaniola with my amazing wife, serving the mission field, and working to equip YOU to live YOUR life of adventure. Since then I have built 3 companies that help support and achieve their dreams and launch their own businesses. I have built websites for billion-dollar companies, partnered with Fortune 500 franchises to profitability, and coached dozens of clients to move from being stuck to being sparked.

And you know what? It all started after I finally took the time to do the REALLY hard stuff; working through my goals. I swear by this process. If you will give it the attention, passion, and focus it deserves.

Let's look at the vision and goals for *'The Top 100 Dream Igniter'* together.

THINGS YOU MUST KNOW ABOUT THE DREAM IGNITER

WELCOME TO 'THE TOP 100 DREAM IGNITER' GOAL-SETTING SYSTEM

This will be the most life-transforming community you will be a part of for the next season of your life.

"Wait a minute! Did you say 'community'?
This is supposed to be a goal-setting tool, right?"

It IS that, but it is so much more.

It is a tool to get onto the mission-development field,
or into any field for that matter.

It is a way to take control of your life and dreams.
It is a method for dealing with obstacles in your life.

It IS all of these things, too. But this guide is so much more!

IT IS A KEY

The *'Top 100'* is a key to a community of people who have been where you have been. Our community is made up of car wash people, coffee baristas, skydivers, workout gurus, not-so-fit people, pastors, 60-year old mothers, fire fighters, students, and more from all over the world. They have each set out to accomplish for themselves what you are going to accomplish with this system.

Our community is made up of every day people from everyday lives from every part of the world who also WANT TO LIVE EXTRAORDINARY LIVES.

Our community serves these people to help them succeed. And we want to partner with you for your success, too!

We have simply termed the community the State of the Spark. This is more than just a state of being sparked for a vision that moves you. It is also a state, a virtual nation, of Spark Citizens who are active, and activating others, in three areas.

Basically, the outcomes for Spark can be viewed as four parts: Life Changes, Community, Global Impact, and deep, Personal Transformation.

I refer to these as **Spark**, **Ignite**, **Explode**, and **Radiate**.

SPARKED VISION: LIFE CHANGES

The Spark vision of life changes is to:

HELP YOU (OUR COMMUNITY) HAVE EFFECTIVE CHANGES IN YOUR LIFE THAT GETS YOU TO WHERE YOU WANT TO GO.

To be sparked is to obtain a vision for more successes and significance in your life. It is your life and there is very little holding you back. So if there is something you want, there is, first and foremost, some goal that should be set and a plan should be implemented to achieve it. We want to help you with that.

We have spent many years studying success material. One of our favorite teachings comes from the ancients!

The ancient Greeks were no dummies. Their schools, known as *paideia*, were based on excellence, *arete*. This typically began with a very strong physical education. Keep in mind that these are the people who gave us the Olympics!

Fitness is a very tangible way to learn the principles of developing habits, and they knew it. As with fitness, any goal demands knowledge, skills, and motivation. If we have these, we will take massive action.

> *"We are what we repeatedly do.*
> *Excellence, then, is not an act, but a habit."*
> – Aristotle

Most gurus and schools of thought suggest that forming habits is a key, integral starting point of life success. With all of these people who have built fortunes suggesting you develop habits, few have offered a pragmatic tool by which to achieve results.

That is the gap we are filling with *'The Top 100 Dream Igniter'* goal-setting system you are holding. It is a pragmatic tool to help you accomplish life changes.

We want to help you create the vision and make the plan necessary to create those effective habits of success for wherever you want to go in life. We want to do that because we know that as you are on the road to excellence it is only a matter of time before you find the one thing that makes all things excellent: community.

> **START SPARKING:** *What is the dream or goal you have had for the longest, but still have not achieved yet?*

_____

_____

_____

_____

_____

_____

IGNITED SUCCESSES: COMMUNITY

The Spark vision for creating ignited successes through the community as it is:

AN UPLIFTING, ENCOURAGING GROUP OF PEOPLE WHO ARE ALL COMMITTED TO HELP EACH OTHER REACH THEIR PERSONAL GOALS.

Igniting successes, lasting successes, is only possible through the interdependent partnering with a powerful community. We want to become interdependent, ignited individuals able to create wins for ourselves and those we affect. In turn, the natural fruit of that will be a powerful community of like-minded people.

After all, how can you truly enjoy success alone?!

I remember hiking to the top of a mountain once when I was in South Africa. It felt great to be up there! I was able to see the Indian Ocean swirling as it met with the Atlantic Ocean, foaming green and blue. It was amazing. But I was missing one thing: the people I loved the most to share it with! Success is like that, sweeter if enjoyed with others.

You may have some sense of satisfaction, but a deep sense of significance and contribution can only come from interacting with a powerful community. The success you seek is seeking you too! It is seeking you in the form of other powerful interdependent, sparked individuals!

We hope that this document gets you on the path to connecting with a sparked community because at that moment, as a unified body, you are perfectly positioned to make a global impact.

EXPLOSIVE SIGNIFICANCE: GLOBAL IMPACT

The Spark vision for making explosive significance through a Global Impact is to:

CREATE GLOBAL IMPROVEMENTS THAT LAST WELL BEYOND OURSELVES, CAUSING AN EXPLOSIVE SENSE OF SIGNIFI-CANCE IN ALL THOSE INVOLVED.

As a sparked community igniting successes in our lives and others, we will experience explosive significance by creating success for others.

Keep in mind; not just any success will do. The successes we create will be major improvements to the quality of life for others. They will be helpful to all involved. And we know that it is inevitable that we will receive benefit, so the focus will be on truly serving others.

This will help more than merely solving immediate challenges. It will create a lasting impact. People will inquire about how they can be sparked. They will seek to partner with the S.o.t.S. community at large to create their own success.

In the end, we will leave the world better off than we found it. And it all starts with where you are at today. Right now. With this guide.

RADIATE PURPOSE: DEEP, PERSONAL TRANSFORMATION

The Spark vision for enabling you to radiate purpose through personal transformation is to:

ENCOURAGE YOU TO TAKE THE TIME TO PROCESS AND SYN-THESIZE THE LESSONS YOU HAVE RECENTLY LEARNED, BE-COME THE PERSON YOU NEED TO BECOME, AND PREPARE YOU FOR THE NEXT SEASON OF SPARKED VISION YOU WILL FACE.

This is the time you put meditation, writing in a journal, and self-reflection to work. In a Radiate season, you slow down, take in less data, and dwell on your recent experiences.

I consider it a "winter" season.

This is when your world rests. You will need to rest up! A renewed sense of "Spring", the next Spark season of Vision, will come soon and will require massive energy.

If you invested well during the Spark, Ignite, and Explode seasons; if you gave it everything you could have, and if you became something better along the way; this should be a powerful season of joy and satisfaction with self.

OUR GOALS FOR YOU WITH THIS SYSTEM

Those are the three major components of the State of the Spark vision. Here are our 3 goals for how *'The Top 100 Dream Igniter'* helps you. That you:

1. Are excited and sparked by the fact that you have a comprehensive action plan for your goals over the next 1 – 3 years.
2. Have identified your Major Definite Purpose.
3. Have a practical system to handle any goal you have now or in the future.

Now that you know what our vision is and what our goals are for how this guide will help you, let's take a look at what is inside it.

We truly believe that what you hold will unlock your life.

So, without further ado, no more excuses, let's do this thing.

Ready? 3... 2... 1... GO!

THE SYSTEM

THE DREAM-IGNITER SYSTEM

INTRODUCTION

How to Approach The Guide, What Is It?, Where Did It Come From?, What is State of the Spark?, Demystifying Motivational Masters, Where 'The Dream Igniter' Fits on Your Spark Journey

PHASE 1 - TOP 100 LIST
Activity: The Download, Different Methods and Tools to Download, What to Do With the Methods and Tools, The Top 100 List

PHASE 2 - CATEGORIZE
How Do You Feel?!, How to Handle Phase 2: Categorize, The Categories, Review Your List

PHASE 3 - A-B-C'S OF GOAL SETTING
Jumping Tracks, Prioritizing, Compare Your Lists, A Final Phase 3 Milestone: Major Definite Purpose

PHASE 4 - 1-YEAR GOALS
Wait, Where Are You At? (A Review), The Little Engine That DOES, You Must Choose, But Choose Wisely, Dreams Determine Destiny and a Little Disenchantment, Long-Term Time Perspective, Giving the Train a Schedule, One More Time For Good Measure, To Infinity and Beyond,

Let's Land This Spaceship, The Train Knows Where to Go

PHASE 5 - GET S.M.A.R.T.
What is SMART?, Your 8 Near-Term Goals But SMART-er, Practice Being Smart, Chugging Along

PHASE 6 - AN ENVIRONMENT FOR SUCCESS
Setting the Stage, Cleaning First, Eliminate Stuff, Wall Calendars, Day-Planner: aka Moleskine, Dream Board, Dream Machine, Your Fortress of Your Fortune, Community, Your Digital World, Digital Calendars: aka Google Calendar, Email, Social Networks, A clean Environment, Well There Is One More Thing,

PHASE 7 - A FREE GIFT
Set a Strategy Session With Me, One More Thing

INTRODUCTION

Chances are that you are familiar with State of the Spark; my approach to coaching, training, and personal-development; or have come across other resources we have created. We still need to cover a few things about *The Dream Igniter* to really get you up and running.

We will dive into the guide in a moment, but taking your time with the Dream Igniter is very important. So, I want to give you an introduction to the document and a brief background on the State of the Spark. Then, we will look at the document together.

HOW TO WIN AT THE TOP 100

As I mentioned on the very first page as well as above, I really want you to take your time with *The Dream Igniter* guide. It is important that you really get your heart, mind, and emotions aligned to the tasks involved here.

To do that, if you have not done so already, print this document off. Seriously! Unless you are already reading *The Top 100 Dream Igniter* in print format, stop now. Send it to the printer or to Staples or wherever.

WHAT IS IT?

This guide is a tool. It is a component of the State of the Spark system.

Don't get me wrong; it is complete within itself. It will accomplish the vision and goals we discussed above. However, you can get even more momentum on your time here if you have already completed *'The 7-Day Spark Homework.' (https://stateofthespark.com/#7-day-hw)*

'The 7-Day Spark Homework' helps prime the creative juices in preparation for *'The Top 100 Dream Igniter'*. Consider it an appetizer that will help you get the most out of your time with this guide.

The Dream Igniter will organize, make you feel confident in your central life direction, and empower you with a system for handling any future goals and vision.

WHERE DID IT COME FROM?

The Dream Igniter has evolved over the last few years.

It was first created for our online success community, SuccessFit. It helped many of the members of SuccessFit get clarity, but it grew when I updated it for my one-on-one life-coaching clients. It was customized again each time I worked with small-business teams to help their partners get personal and organizational clarity.

Now the State of the Spark and our community is building momentum around personal success and translating your passion into action, often in the form of building a small business or organization. (I often say that entrepreneurship is the economic system for those seeking freedom.)

This is the tool you have in your hands today.

WHAT IS THE STATE OF THE SPARK?

The State of the Spark is a model I have used for the past few years. As I struggled for better and better language to describe a tangible process for intangible growth, State of the Spark kept lighting me up.

The model is simple yet potent.

Spark your Vision.

Ignite your Success.

Explode your Significance.

The fourth stage, **Radiate**, is a far more personal one.

Radiate your Purpose.

We do that by fusing with others by fusing with God.

(I strongly believe that as you move through life and become more enlightened about your ability to discover and act toward vision, to create successes for yourself, and to turn those insights toward helping others; that a revelation of the Divine is inevitable. I focus on the first three, because we can begin to take action on these right away.)

DEMYSTIFYING MOTIVATIONAL MASTERS

If you study any of the motivational masters, they each have their own system. State of the Spark is mine. Each of the systems that teachers have used throughout time, however, are quite similar. To explain this simply, I have created an informational graphic for you to look over. Check it out here: www.StateoftheSpark.com and look under *Resources* for The Grid of Success.

As you can see from *The Grid of Success*, I believe that all of the new gurus and fancy systems out there are pointing to age-old truths.

"The elevator to the top is out of order, but the stairs are always open."
- Zig Ziglar

Just like these gurus who were sharing these truths in a relevant way

THE GRID OF SUCCESS
Demystifying Motivational Masters

State of the Spark	spark	ignite	explode	radiate	notes
Grant R. Nieddu	vision	success	significance	purpose	
Ancient Greece	mind (psuche)		character	spirit (pneuma) - peace with gods	
Maslow's Needs	physical		social & love	self-actualized & peak experiences	
Joseph Campbell	departure	initiation	return (to rescue from without)	return (return threshold - end)	
Steven Covey	private victories	public victories	interdependence	sharpening the saw	
Steven Covey	to live	to learn	to love	to leave a legacy	
Napoleon Hill	desire, faith & autosuggestion	specialized knowledge, imagination & decision	persistence, mastermind & love	subconscious, the brain & the 6th sense	
Tony Robbins	principles & state mastery		significance, connection & love	contribute beyond oneself	
Seasons	spring	summer	fall	winter	
Hope	healthy relationships	optimism	persistence	energy, effort, enthusiasm	
Apprenticeship	apprentice	journeyman	master	grandmaster	
(other applications)					
Childhood Creativity	interests		explore	awe	
Simon Sinek	why		how		
Robert Kyosaki	employee	self-employed	business owner	investor	

to their immediate audience, State of the Spark is my presentation of it for people to understand today.

I have attempted to simplify the process without taking any shortcuts. There are no shortcuts. There is just the hard work of making changes from the inside out.

WHERE THE DREAM IGNITER BELONGS ON YOUR SPARK JOURNEY

If *'The 7-Day Spark Homework'* falls in the beginning of the Spark phase of personal life success, then this guide falls toward the end of the Spark phase and helps bridge you to take action in the Ignite phase.

There are more teachings about the Spark method of igniting a life of explosive life of significance at www.StateoftheSpark.com. If you cannot find what you are looking for there, please find me at GrantNieddu.com to answer any questions you have.

Phew! That was a lot.

- *At this point, you have slowed down and taken your time.*
- *You have placed your fears about the future aside. Whether you have fear of not accomplishing your goals or fear of accomplishing your goals, these fears are put to the side for now.*
- *You have printed off this entire document.*
- *You have read over the entire document to understand the overview.*

Along with that, you have learned about *'The Top 100 Dream Igniter'*, the State of the Spark and become familiar about *The Dream Igniter's* role on your own spark journey toward a passionate life.

I think that is all you need to know to get started quickly! Let's begin!

"The way to get started is to quit talking and begin doing."

– WALT DISNEY

PHASE 1:

TOP 100 LIST

Estimated Time:	Just Sparking Out: Allow 2 – 4 hours of thoughtful time in your favorite coffee shop. Take your time. This is not a race. It demands thoughtful introspection.
Approach:	Review the section over entirely one time first without writing anything. Return to this spot and read it line by line. Then begin the activity.
What We Will Cover:	Understand how categorizing fits in the train model. Have organized your items in a way that increases the chance of success.

Your 'Top 100' is a VERY important step to setting and achieving your goals. Below you will find 100 spaces.

THE DOWNLOAD

As a fore-warning, this is more challenging than it first seems.

Many people think that it will be easy. Writing the first 10 – 20 goals is fairly easy. The next 30 – 40 keep flowing, but begin to taper off. Then they begin to stall out on things to write around the 50 or 60 mark.

BUT, that is where it gets really interesting!

At that point, other parts of your brain begin to wake up. Your mind begins to dig deep. You start to renew all of those dreams you had as a young person. Once you pass 65 or 70, your mind will be flowing freely, and you will not be able to stop the flow of dreams and desires that you have!

If 'The Top 100 Dream Igniter' is a bullet train to your dreams, The Download is Grand Central Station.

The Download is where all of your ideas gather. All those thoughts in your head gather, pass each other without recognizing one another (though they probably went to school together), and look generally chaotic.

But, those ideas in your mind are trying to get somewhere. They are all looking for the right station and checking their clock for the right departure time. Each idea carries its own baggage, has its own aspirations, and thinks it is the center of the universe.

However, you are the one looking into the Grand Central. You know each thought intimately. If you tried to focus on just one at a time, you would be exhausted.

But you are the Grand Conductor. Each dream and idea IS important. And you will experience the sights, sounds and tastes of each destination.

However, in *The Download* you have to get in the crowd. You have to ask each and every traveler who they are, where they are going, and give them a ticket.

Later in the guide we will organize the ideas (when we organize them, rank them, and strategize them.) For now we are simply going to ticket them; we are going to give each thought and emotion its own place on the list.

Once that's done, the chaos of the Grand Central Station in your heart and mind will look like organized chaos. You will be able to better identify who is going where.

So, let's get busy and download.

DIFFERENT METHODS AND TOOLS

The principle of *The Download* is simple: write down each thought. (See, I told you it was simple.)

There is only 1 rule: Just flow. (See! 1 principle and 1 rule. That's it.) Said another way, Rule 1: 'Just flow' means do not organize them.

Do not stop to put this one next to that one because it's similar to another one. Resist the temptation. Just let your mind jump from synapse to the next synapse, from connectome to connectome, to thought to thought.

As I have done this with dozens of people, we have found a variety of ways to get the brain flowing.

Mind-mapping: One way to download is a mind-map. You probably did this in grade school, a little in high school, and, if you were old enough to get some loans before the Credit Crunch, you might have done this in college, too.

Mind-mapping is great for the following reasons. A.) You can get all your thoughts out. B.) Those thoughts can be seen at once while beginning to show signs of valuable connections. C.) You can easily organize your ideas now that they are out.

There are digital mind-mapping tools. MindManager, LucidChart and FreeMind are all helpful tools for mind-mapping. Of the digital ways to mind-map, I prefer FreeMind. It is a free piece of software, easy to install and easy to use (once you figure out the keyboard shortcuts.)

Mind-mapping on paper is helpful and makes my brain feel great! In fact, mind-mapping on paper is my preferred method of mind-mapping. Not only does it accomplish the reasons listed above, but it makes the ideas more tangible.

Here are the mind-mapping tools for doing it by hand.

- *Individual Slips of Paper* – You can get this going anywhere, any time. Be sure you have a way to store and file all of those random slips of paper, though!
- *Post-Its* – These are the best mistaken invention 3M ever had! I get

down to business with Post-Its. Find them. Use them. Let your brain pump out ideas a plenty with Post-Its. I also like them because if you are using a table, they won't blow around. And if you are using a wall,.. well, you can use a wall!

- *Index Card* – These are good because you can write the amorphous idea on the blank side and write the details on the lined side. They are also all the same size and fit neatly into those plexi cube boxes to store.
- *Sharpie* – Use a fat sharpie. The reason for this is that you are forced to write single, thick words. With a fine tool like a pen, you may be tempted to write out details. Avoid this tendency. Write big words. Fill up that sticky note or index card so you can read it from across the room.
- *Music with no lyrics.* This is crucial. Music with lyrics will consciously and unconsciously trigger thought patterns, and those may not all be helpful or positive.

You want to have creative flow. You want your brain to really get pumping without the influence of other people's ideas. So, choose your preferred music style, and find your favorite playlist with no lyrics and go to town.

You could do speed metal, electronica, dubstep, or classical. Whatever gets your creative juices flowing!

WHAT TO DO WITH THE METHODS

Once you choose your approach, sit down and get to business. Grab that coffee or tea, put on your selected music, and just unleash. Make it a moment to remember, but this is when your desires go from chaos to corralled.

Just before we begin, I want you to visualize this. I want you to imagine that this is the moment that you validate everyone in Grand Central Station running around like crazy. This is the moment that they at least know where everything in the train station is and that you are safely watching over them.

ACTIVITY: CAPTURE THE DOWNLOAD

Now, set that timer, get cozy and go, go, go!!! Let's do this. 3... 2... 1... GO

STOP NOW!
Find your tools and get to business.
See you in a few hours!!

ACTIVITY: CAPTURE THE TOP 100 LIST

Start Sparking! Transfer your Top 100 list of things you want to do, see, and be here!

1 _____

2 _____

3 _____

4 _____

5 _____

6 _____

7 _____

8 _____

9 _____

10 _____

11 _____

12 _____
13 _____
14 _____
15 _____
16 _____
17 _____
18 _____
19 _____
20 _____
21 _____
22 _____
23 _____
24 _____
25 _____
26 _____
27 _____
28 _____
29 _____
30 _____
31 _____
32 _____
33 _____
34 _____
35 _____
36 _____

37 _____
38 _____
39 _____
40 _____
41 _____
42 _____
43 _____
44 _____
45 _____
46 _____
47 _____
48 _____
49 _____
50 _____
51 _____
52 _____
53 _____
54 _____
55 _____
56 _____
57 _____
58 _____
59 _____
60 _____
61 _____

62 _____
63 _____
64 _____
65 _____
66 _____
67 _____
68 _____
69 _____
70 _____
71 _____
72 _____
73 _____
74 _____
75 _____
76 _____
77 _____
78 _____
79 _____
80 _____
81 _____
82 _____
83 _____
84 _____
85 _____
86 _____

87 _____
88 _____
89 _____
90 _____
91 _____
92 _____
93 _____
94 _____
95 _____
96 _____
97 _____
98 _____
99 _____
100 _____
101 _____
102 _____
103 _____
104 _____
105 _____
106 _____
107 _____
108 _____
109 _____
110 _____

Welcome Back!!!

How do you feel?!! Phew! Take a breath. Get up and stretch. Take a quick walk. But come back soon because we need to wrap this up!

Once you have done 100, do another few. (My prediction is that you may have more than that!) You should have what looks like a mess of paper slips, or spidery-webbed digital mind-map, or a filled out legal pad, in front of you. They may be chaotic, but you should feel a touch of excitement in your stomach seeing all of your dreams right there in front of you.

Now, in no particular order or sequence, pick up the nearest one and write in in the first blank provided. (The repetition of writing your ideas and dreams down is meant to reinforce positive neuro-chemical stimulation, so just do it!) Place it behind you, or in a folder or in a plexi box. Whichever you use, get it out of sight and move on to the next one.

CONGRATULATIONS!!

That was a huge accomplishment! Notice there are 110, not just 100, spots! You want to be an overachiever, don't you!

Now, do us a favor: Go to StateoftheSpark.com/top100 (OR, our Facebook group,

The Goals and Gratitude Group
https://www.facebook.com/groups/stateofthespark),

and tell us in the comments:

"I FINISHED MY GOALS!"

Seriously! Do it. I dub thee Sparked Visionary. You have leveled up to someone who has acknowledged and taken serious direction toward the vision(s) in their heart.

Writing out your goals and dreams is something that only 13% of the population will ever do. You are NOW officially part of the top 13%. In the world of fitness, this is like completing a half-marathon.

So, celebrate!

"Wait!" I can hear you say. *"Why is it only like a 'half' marathon?"*

Because we have only begun, and there is a marathon to complete!

REFLECTIONS

Write down any other observations or brainstorms here:

*"Men admire
the man who
can organize
their wishes and
thoughts in stone
and wood and
steel and brass."*

– RALPH WALDO EMERSON

CATEGORIZE

Estimated Time:	Just Sparking Out: Allow 2 – 4 hours of thoughtful time in your favorite coffee shop. Take your time. This is not a race. It demands thoughtful introspection..
Preparation:	Needed Items: A pen or pencil. The Guide.
Approach:	Review the section over entirely one time first without writing anything. Return to this spot and read it line by line. Then begin the activity.
What We Will Cover:	Understand how categorizing fits in the train model. Have organized your items in a way that increases the chance of success. Decide if any goals begin to stick out as possibly unlocking success for others.

HOW DO YOU FEEL?! EXCITED??!

I hope you do, because I know I did the first time I did this. It actually took me a whole weekend. At first it was like pulling teeth. Then it started to flow. By Sunday night I was exhausted and thrilled!!

Usually people find a great sense of relief just writing all of those dreams down. They have been holding the chaos of their goals inside for so long that once it is totally written out, they are ready to crash as if they had just finished a full marathon. Sadly, they usually stop there.

DO NOT STOP THERE.

You are not off the hook. Remember, *The Download* phase was only a half-marathon!

We are going to get some steam behind that list. We are going to categorize the goals to get a better handle on how to strategize them.

Now that all of those ideas are written, we can begin to get them on the right track. That starts by placing them together. If you were in the Grand Central Station of your thoughts, ideas, and desires, this moment is the moment that you have the attention of everyone in the station.

Phase 2: Categorize is the moment where you go through the crowd and check everyone's ticket. Glancing at their ticket, you direct them to other travelers with the same destination. We are not pointing them to a train just yet! We are simply gathering them with other travelers headed in the same direction.

What this means for your Top 100 is that you will review the list of your *Download* of your 100 items and think about them for a moment. Where does each one fit? Where should it be placed?

HOW TO CATEGORIZE

Below are a series of preset categories. Read over the titles of each of them before you begin. Ask yourself if you need to add another category or if you need to get rid of one.

I have offered you 10 spots for each category. Be bold! Do not be afraid to limit it to ten or to add another to fill up the 10! This is not the time to edit your list. It is simply the moment to categorize it.

If you need more spots for a category, write them off to the side. Leave some of the blanks unfilled if you just do not have that many.

There is no pressure to fit the mold. There is just flow!

Give yourself a few hours to write them in. Move on here or there. Add or subtract categories. Along the way, visualize accomplishing each one as you write it in its place. Take a second to imagine that thing being obtained, that characteristic being exuded, that goal being accomplished in your own life.

Let's go!

ACTIVITY: CATEGORIZATION!

Character Development

_____

_____

_____

_____

_____

Spiritual

_____

_____

_____

_____

_____

Mental & Emotional

_____

_____

_____

_____

_____

Physical Fitness

_____

_____

_____

_____

_____

Passion & Lifestyle

_____

_____

_____

_____

_____

Relational & Community

_____

_____

_____

_____

_____

Organization or Cause

_____

_____

_____

_____

Adventure & Travel

_____

_____

_____

_____

_____

BOOM!
All of your ideas are starting to heat up!

And you have leveled up to an Apprentice Sparked Strategist!

It is more than merely writing down your visions, it is beginning to make decisions toward their accomplishment.

Imagine the travelers in your train station talking with each other in groups. They are saying things like, "oh, you are going to such-and-such a place? Me, too!" They are exchanging ideas about places to visit, restaurants to sample, and people to meet.

This is a point of momentum-building for your ideas. This is where ideas that correlate begin to make more sense to you in groups. You may have a hint at how they could connect and work together. You may begin to see how a certain action will complete two or three of them at a time.

REVIEW THE CATEGORIZED LISTS

In a particular category, do you see how one course of action could accomplish multiple goals?

_____

Which category is it?

_____

What items could you accomplish?

_____

What course of action could accomplish them?

_____

_____

_____

_____

Look at several other categories. Do you see similar approaches to succeeding at other items? What thoughts or brainstorms do you have that could knock out more than two or three items if you succeeded at it?

Which category is it?

_____

What items could you accomplish?

_____

What course of action could accomplish them?

_____

_____

_____

_____

REFLECTIONS

Write down any other observations or brainstorms here:

"If you don't prioritize yourself, you constantly start falling lower and lower on your list."

– MICHELLE OBAMA

EASY AS A-B-C

Estimated Time:	Allow 3+ hours
Preparation:	Needed Items: A pen or pencil. The Guide.
Approach:	Review Phase 3 entirely one time first without writing anything. Return to this spot and read it line by line. Then begin the activity.
What We Will Cover:	Understanding the Rating system. Rate your goals in Phase 1. Review. Rate your goals in Phase 2. Compare the ratings from Phase 1 and Phase 2. Identify your MDP.

You have conquered the first two major challenges to living an intentionally outstanding life! Just getting them out of your head and validating your ideas was a huge first step. And then, to organize them and start to put them together were steps to being a true strategist.

Now comes some of the nitty-gritty meat of goal setting: Rating your list!

This is not for the faint of heart. This is where you have to tell some things they are first and other things that, well, they may just have to wait.

Do not rush this! It will take some very real soul searching. Compare this to walking through the groups in your Grand Central Station of ideas. They know where they are headed in general. They are in groups of similar travelers and waiting patiently while they talk amongst themselves. They are waiting for you, the Station Director and Goal-Train Conductor to tell them when it is their turn.

This is the moment where you will walk through those marbled-floored halls and address each of them to tell them who is getting on the first car, who is getting on the second car, and third and so on. You will have to break the news to those who will have to be in a later car, but here is what you can say to those ideas and desires of yours.

"Never fear! By ensuring the success of the first things, I am increasing the likelihood that we will accomplish the later things!"

And it is the truth. By going through and prioritizing the most important things (and I will show you how to decide that below) you are giving your other goals the real chance they deserve.

Here is how that works.

JUMPING TRACKS

If you go through life, jumping from one dream to the next trying to knock them out, you just may accomplish a good handful of things. In all likelihood, however, there will be many things that will remain undone.

What's worse, in our lives we really are on only one train. This is what is crazy about your Grand Central Station of ideas: there is only one train, and one track.

When people are in the later years of their lives, they look back and realize the beauty and tragedy of this fact. It is beautiful that life really only has one track, because what feels like chaos, in hindsight, turns out to be a truly beautiful, divinely-ordained adventure. It is also a tragedy because they often think that if they had identified it early, realized that life was leading them in one direction, they would have prioritized the things that really matter. They realize that the act of prioritizing would ensure success in the other areas because it would ensure success on the deepest, most fulfilling things first.

Thankfully, you are here right now making that great decision so many others only wished they had made when they were your age.

ACTIVITY: PRIORITIZING

Here is how we will rank the items on your list. You will go through your Top 100 list twice.

The first time, I want you to jump back to Phase 1: The Download. Review the A, B, C, D, and E ranking system below. Then, starting wherever you want on that first list, begin ranking them according to the rating system below.

You will rank them with an "A", "B", "C", "D", or "E".

- **Things that you know you could never live without accomplishing get an "A".** These are things that you would like to have written on your grave stone. They are the things you want to be known for; the legacy you wish to leave. One of my "A" list items is to live a life of missions. BAM! No can take that away.
- **Things that you greatly desire to be, do, or have, and really do wish to accomplish, but could see yourself doing them in the later years of your life get a "B".** My "B" list example would be owning a nice home with a study and library. I really want to have that hovel, that place I can study and write. But it just isn't in my make-up right now.
- **"C" things are things that you really could live without.** They may bring you happiness or some mild sense of fulfillment, but you really could die not having done them. The best example for me for C things is running for political office. I am greatly interested in doing it. But I really could pass away and not feel bad about it.
- **Things that should just get delegated get a "D".** These are things that you need to do but just do not want to do them yourself. You

could delegate these things by paying someone else, obtaining volunteers or creating partnerships, or finding your own elves to finish them. Examples may be website development. (Stay focused on content creation.) Or incorporating your non-profit. (Can you have your ministry interns check into it?)

- **Everything else, those things that should just be eliminated, get an "E".** These are things that are frail and paper-thin. An example for me was that I had on my list "I own a Mclaren SLR". After a while of staring at that thing, I just erased it.

PRIORITIZING STEP 1

Flip back to Phase 1: the Download, in the Top 100 list. It may take you a while. That is fine. Grab a protein shake, kick your sneakers up, turn your ball cap around, and DO THIS NOW.

STOP NOW.
Turn back to Phase 1 and GET TO BUSINESS!
See you in a bit!!

How was that?! Was it easier or more difficult than your original Download of the Top 100? Was it easier or more difficult than Phase 2: Categorize?

WERE THERE ANY ITEMS THAT TOOK LARGE AMOUNTS OF TIME TO DELIBERATE? WRITE THEM DOWN:

_____

_____

_____

_____

_____

PRIORITIZING STEP 2

Speaking of Phase 2: Categorize, as we said before, we are actually going _to do this activity again!_

Yes, that is right. We are going to make a second pass at categorizing these things. Bear with me on this. _Keep reading because this is important._

Last time we did this in Phase 1. Now, we are going to do this for _the second time_, but with Phase 2: Categorize. The reason for this is that I want you to really evaluate for a second time how you feel about things.

Seeing each item next to other items may provide additional perspective. Next to similar items, something that was a "B" may look like a paltry "C". That "D" may take on new inspiration for you to become a "B".

So, without trying to recreate or refer to the last list, _I want you to flip to Phase 2: Categorize and begin ranking!_

STOP NOW.
Turn back to Phase 2and GET TO BUSINESS!
See you in Another Quick Moment!!

Phew! What an accomplishment.

Head over to www.StateoftheSpark.com/top100 and I want you to post a quick note:

"I PRIORITIZED MY GOALS!!"

Now that you have written, categorized, and prioritized your goals, I declare that you are a Journeyman Sparked Strategist. This is a true level-up.

You have been able to give your visions credibility as a Sparked Visionary. As an Apprentice Sparked Strategist, you began nudging your Top 100 items around in small decisions.

Today, you have made HUGE decisions about them. You have made decisions that will affect when you take massive, real-world action in their direction.

CONGRATULATIONS!
You are KILLING it.

To get absolute assurance that these are your items, however, we are going to compare them.

PRIORITIZING STEP 3: COMPARE YOUR LISTS

To get further clarity, I want you to compare lists. Using Phase 2: Categorize as your primary reference, I want you to go down your list one at a time.

1. Find the first item on your Phase 2 list.
2. Find the same item on your Phase 1 list.
3. Then, on the Phase 2 list, next to the ranking you already wrote down, I want you to write down the ranking you gave yourself on the Phase 1 list.
4. Repeat for each item on the Phase 2 list.

Can you see what we are doing here?? We are solidifying some things. We are getting clarity about what you *really* want. (I am assuming you neither attempted to recreate the first pass nor referred to it when making the second pass.)

Those things that have two "A"s next to them. You can be pretty sure these are very important to you. Those things that have two "E"s, please, for all of our sakes, eliminate them from you mind. Do you see how this worked?!

Now, about those things that have a "C" and a "B" next to them, leave them alone for now. We really want clarity on what are some of the things that are in stone for you.

MAJOR DEFINITE PURPOSE: A FINAL PHASE 3 MILESTONE

We are going to do a small exercise.

This will not demand a lot of writing such as the last few Phases have. This will likely take massive amounts of introspection.

I want you to look at your double "A" items. These are the things (or maybe just the one thing?) that you ranked as a top priority during both passes of this exercise.

I want you to dwell on those things. I want you to imagine yourself having them, being those characteristics, or seeing those projects accomplished.

What emotions do they give you? Do they create excitement?! I mean, really imagine and day-dream about having those things happen! At that moment, how would you feel???

Now let me ask you this question: which of them stands out as a beacon of electric light to your heart?

Does one in particular make your hand stand on end? If I could write a check or wave a wand and make one, and only one of them come to pass, do you know which one it would be?

This is your *Major Definite Purpose*. This is the center of your Life of Mission. This is the reason for your Sparked Journey on the Earth.

WRITE IT HERE:

_____

_____

_____

_____

_____

_____

ASK YOURSELF THESE QUESTIONS:

Do you like the idea that this thing is your Major Definite Purpose?

_____

_____

Are you ok telling people this is the center of your Life Mission?

_____

_____

Is it inspiring enough to fuel your Sparked Journey?

_____

_____

Can you see how moving toward your Major Definite Purpose would unlock so many of your other goals?

_____

_____

Get total clarity on this thing, because the rest of *The Top 100* guide will revolve around this.

If the answer to any of the questions above was "No", I am going to encourage you to stop right here and now. If you do not like the fact that you are excited or moved by what you wrote just now, I urge you to do some serious soul-searching to find out why you do not like it.

Perhaps you wrote that you want to be a multimillionaire. Perhaps that gets you electrically excited. Yet, when I asked the questions that followed, you realized that you do not want to tell people that this is your Life Mission.

I would listen to that still, small voice that caused you to take pause. (There is nothing wrong with that being a *Major Definite Purpose*, a Sparked Journey. But if you don't like that fact, then there is disintegration.)

Take just a quick moment and watch this video on Integration. I cannot get enough of this teaching from Jim Rohn about integrity: https://youtu.be/IrAKOJxicuA.

If you wrote down a *Major Definite Purpose*, a Sparked Vision, a Mission for Life, AND you can now answer "Yes" to the questions that follow, I have to say:

*You have leveled up
to being an IGNITED SUCCESS.*

*You, where you stand, right now, are a radiating,
pulsating bundle of electric, ignited success!!*

You are a success as you are today! You know your central purpose! You are in a club that few ever will be!

I wish you could feel how completely excited and happy for you I am right now!! You have crossed a threshold that you will never be able to come back from! You may have highs and lows, but you can always return to this moment and remind yourself that there is one thing (and likely more) that stir you up to excitement and fulfillment in every cell of your being.

We have to celebrate!!

I want you to go to our website and on that same page, tell me that you are an Ignited Success!!

Do it now! Do it for me! Do it for others considering getting clarity for their goals!

Next, I want you to call your closest confidant and tell them how excited you are. Share your joy with them.

Finally, to make a milestone of this moment, I want you to find an index card. On that index card I want you to write down your MDP, your major definite purpose. It should be in the present-progressive tense.

And I want you to carry it with you wherever you go. I want it to be in your pocket or your purse. Every time you touch it I want you to imagine lightning moving through your hand, through your arm, into your mind and lighting your brain up. I want it to cause you to smile.

And I hope you're smiling because you know something that few, if anyone, know. You have the secret that has made millionaires and nation-shakers. It is to know one's purpose for living.

Phew! I am freaking out for you!

If you have an index card, do it now. If not, then take a moment to fill out the certificate on the next page. Feel free to cut this out or tear it out and tape it to your wall.

Now, choose a realistic, attainable date for completing this goal. Do NOT put the date too far away, though. Remember, Parkinson's Law states that "work expands to fill the time allotted".

That means that if you tell yourself it will take 2 years, it will take 2 years. If you tell yourself it will take 6 months, it will take six months.

So, in the space below, write out your *Major Definite Purpose* with the date. Use the PRESENT, PERSONAL, and POSITIVE tense of any verbs. (Use, "I HAVE" instead of "I will have." "I AM" instead of "I will be".)

Look at it first thing in the morning and last thing at night! Look at it at lunch when no one's looking! Make a habit of touching it, reading it out loud, and allowing it to excite your mind.

My Major Definite Purpose is that I:

_____

_____

_____

And I here and now commit to any ethical service necessary for its attainment by this date:

_____

Signed: _____

REFLECTIONS

Write down any other observations or brainstorms here:

"You were born to win, but to be a winner, you must plan to win, prepare to win, and expect to win."

– ZIG ZIGLAR

1-YEAR GOALS

Estimated Time:	Allow 3.5+ hours, but take your time if it needs more.
Preparation:	Needed Items: A pen or pencil. The Guide. (And probably coffee; this is a long exercise!)
Approach:	Review Phase 4 entirely one time first without writing anything. Return to this spot and read it line by line. Then begin the activity.
What We Will Cover:	Setting your 1 year goals and how to set milestones for each item.

REVIEW: WAIT, WHERE ARE WE AT?

You have come a long way. You started out becoming a Sparked Visionary and, so far, have ended up an Ignited Success. You went from little clarity to total clarity. What's more, you should have a pretty good idea what is most important to you (your Major Definite Purpose), the priority of all the things you want to do, and, thus, the beginnings of a solid strategy.

Well, here is where things really get specific. This is where you see if the things you have defined for yourself are really the things you want. The reason is that this phase, Phase 4, is where you get to see what it actually takes. *This phase is where you start thinking strategically.*

This is where we grind it out; where you have to wake early, stay up later, push harder and invest more to accomplish the priorities in your heart. But, I believe that you can do it. And I believe that you are more likely to commit yourself to the day-in and day-out grind because you can see where this is leading you.

THE LITTLE ENGINE THAT DOES!

What about the other travelers in your train station, those other ideas still on the list? You know, the other 99 things we discovered that you wanted?

They are still hanging around where you told them last. They are in groups, waiting for your instructions. This is the moment where you, the Conductor of Ideas, look at the one train you have and start getting a concept of who gets seated in the front, middle or back.

As the Conductor, very familiar with the train's engine (yourself and all you are capable of), you know that each idea, each group of people have a First Class ticket. They will all get the top-notch treatment, the special attention that only you can give. You know that you are going to give 100% to whatever you put your hands too. That is a given.

What you are pondering is simply who gets that attention first. Where will the train stop first? Where will you direct the engine to take you and your worthy ideas?

This is where we decide to put all of our steam and fire and strength for the next little while, confident that we will arrive
at our destination.

YOU MUST CHOOSE, BUT CHOOSE WISELY

Our first stop is similar to the other stops in that it is a destination of success. But which destination first? How do you decide?

In thinking about our first goal or series of goals, we know a few things. From my time with life-coaching, I can tell you that often people miscalculate their abilities.

Some are unsure of themselves, so they only focus on single, short-term goals. The problem is there is very little sense of fulfillment or excitement to keep them going. Opposite of that are the coaching clients

I have had who dream way too big too soon! This creates massive frustration because the person feels they are not making any progress.

Brian Tracy has said:

> *We greatly overestimate what we can accomplish in one year but underestimate what we can accomplish in three years.*

What he is getting at emphasizes this point. We do not dream big enough over the longer term. We dream too darn big over the short term.

DREAMS DETERMINE DESTINY, & A LITTLE DISENCHANTMENT

Most people are in the habit of creating year long goals. Then, when they do not accomplish it, there is this sense of defeat. *"Oh, well, I didn't do it. Life is over."* It is almost as if the world ceases to exist in our planning beyond a year.

We have to bridge together the short-term goals with the long-term goals.

LONG-TERM TIME PERSPECTIVE

I once worked for a millionaire real estate developer who reminded me that *"Time is the currency of the wealthy."*

This has very many applications, but we will focus on the fact that to become a success you must be a master at managing the 'currency of the wealthy.' We must be master-strategists with time.

> *Odd Principle: You cannot manage time. You can only manage yourself.*

What the millionaire was teaching me in one sense is the need to manage one's self and one's actions in an organized, disciplined fashion to attain the goal in a given time.

You can never manage time. You can only manage yourself.

GIVING THE TRAIN A SCHEDULE

How this looks for us, master-strategists for success at our goals, is that we will keep one eye on our long-term goals but focus our attention and effort on short-term goals. Those short-term goals will be building toward near-term goals, things that are just challenging and out-of-reach enough to stretch us. The near-term goals will also be chunks of larger, long-term dreams that we would never typically think we could accomplish.

A near-term goal is between short-term and long-term goals. A short-term goal would be something to accomplish in the next few days, weeks or months. A long-term goal is something to accomplish in the next 2-4 years, 3-5 years, or 5-10 years.

A near-term goal is something to accomplish in the next 6 – 18 months (but specifically avoids the 12 month mark, you know, to break that paradigm.)

A) The Logical Order Overview

Look over your items.

Does there seem to be a logical order to them? Usually we find out there is.

Say that one of your goals is that you want to live in Cancun. And, for example, let's say another one of your goals is that you want to have $100,000 in the bank. Now, even though living in Cancun really doesn't cost all that much, it would make logical sense to make some decent money first. Besides, if you went to Cancun first and left your community, job and network back home, making $100,000 profit while just getting by in Mexico would require starting from scratch. It would not be impossible, you would have just made it all the more challenging for yourself.

So, a possible logical order would be that putting the $100,000 in the bank comes before living in Cancun. (It would make sense that earning money or building a stream of income is the key goal to unlocking most of the others.)

To give you a real example, for Marissa and I to make our transition to living in the Dominican Republic, we had a dollar goal for money in the bank. It was a small enough number we could reach it in 1 or 2 years, but big enough to stretch our thinking and sustain us on the field for about 18 months.

As we progressed, our hard work earned much of the goal, but serendipity and putting our vision in front of others caused an additional 50% more than our goal to achieve it. We got married within the same time frame and, because of our value of frugality for the vision, we came out ahead!

This gave us a great head start to knocking out several of our dreams.

Going back to our example of moving to Cancun, we now have a question before us. (Forming the right question usually brings about the right answers.) The question is:

How do I make $100,000 dollars?

Once we ask "how," we just need to break it down. Without asking whether or not we can, simply break down earning an additional $100,00. Seriously, it is very rare that you will wake up one day to find that extra money just sitting in your account!

B) Bite-Sized Chunks

Near-term and Long-term goals are merely the accumulation of an intentional sequence of short-term goals. Most people live one short-term goal to the next with very little overarching plan behind them.

In terms of your train, this is like the train going to its first destination, then turning back and returning to the station to pick up other travelers. The momentum of the train is lost, the direction has gotten all turned around, and the second travelers will arrive at their destinations quite late.

But master-strategists don't do that! They think it through first, load up the train, and send it down the tracks confident in the uniformity of direction! We just have to break it down into small chunks.

Let me show you what I mean.

You could break the $100,000 down to chunks of questions. Begin by answering the question of *"how do I make $10,000"*, or *"how do I make $25,000"*, or *"how do I earn an extra $1,667 a month for five years."* You could do this math pretty easily.

If moving to Cancun is a 5-year goal, and you want to find that extra $100,000, that is earning an extra $20,000 a year. Or, it is earning an extra $1,667 a month!

You could put the move to Cancun first by forming the right question:

How can I move to Cancun, and still be positioned to earn $100,000 or more in the next 5 years?

This would then get the Chunk Treatment. Name the components of the move first:

"How do I find a frugal place to live?", *"How do I save the money for a plane ticket?"*, *"Who do I know that has already lived in Cancun?"*, *"What work can I do or business can I build living in Cancun?"*, and on.

Then, consider the $100,000 in your line of questioning. *"How can I move to Cancun and maintain, or expand, my network?"*, *"What groups of business-owners, entrepreneurs, or Americans are currently living in Cancun whom I can serve?"*

The creativity to form questions goes on and on!

But, I know that this may be a stretch to believe that you can earn that kind of money on a regular basis or make a transition that big when you consider where you are at right now. So, let's not consider where we are at right now! Let's consider where we could be!

Einstein said:

You cannot answer a question at the same level of thinking you had when you asked it.

C) Expand Your Thinking

So, you have a solid idea of how big the goal is, and you know that you have to expand your belief. Let's answer a second important question:

How do I expand my knowledge and, therefore, my belief so that I can earn an extra $100,000?

What do you do to expand your belief? READ. Study. Model millionaires. Find examples of people who made an extra $100,000 and do what they did.

And you can see our "plan" forming, just by asking the right questions.

D) Identify the Plan

Start by writing down what you have gathered so far. Here is what it would look like:

> *To make $100,000, I need to a) know what others have done to earn this and more, b) do what they have done, so I need to c) plan it out.*

(I think a good model would be to just spend the first 6 months STUDYING! Then, you will have more knowledge to base the next four and a half years on.)

That leads you to your near-term goals for the next 18 months to begin earning $100,000. It would go something like this:

1. Read 10 books by or about millionaires.
2. Interview 1 wealthy person over coffee or lunch each month.
3. Write a plan based on the information gathered.
4. Initiate the plan.
5. Earn an additional $10,000 from working extra and being frugal.

(I say only $10,000 the first 18 months because, as you will find, riches compound. Once you earn $10,000, earning the next $50,000 becomes easier. Then, earning $100,000 is a cinch.)

That sounds far-fetched, I know, but it's true. The same is true for losing weight.

1. Read 3 books about losing weight.
2. Interview 1 person who has lost weight or has helped someone lose weight.

3. Write a plan based on the information gathered.
4. Initiate the plan.
5. Lose first 10 pounds from adding basic, consistent exercise and eating what you know you should.

ONE MORE TIME FOR GOOD MEASURE

Let's look at the same process we took for the $100,000 and apply it to something not related to money. Often my coaching clients would look at money and would say, *"Yeah, you can do that math pretty easy because it's numbers. But how does this look for something you have no idea about?"*

It's all the same process. Let's look.

To Infinity, and Beyond!

As a kid, I always wanted to go to space. I had a waterbed with a huge space mural over it. I would sit on my water-bed, floating and bobbing, and pretend I was floating in space.

So, let's pretend that your goal is to go to space. (For me, it's not a stretch of my imagination at all! I would seriously LOVE IT!!)

In the past, the path was pretty clear.

1. Enter the Air Force.
2. Become a stellar pilot and get a related degree.
3. Apply to the Space Program.
4. And apply again. And apply again.

All in all, it was simple, clear, and would take about 15 to 20 years of your life. (Hey, big goals take big investments.)

Along the way you have your meals taken care of, earn a really nice G.I. Bill, and get to travel the world. (It IS the military so that is some risk involved.)

But space travel has changed.

We no longer consistently go to the moon and have basically exited the Space Race. I am not a rocket scientist (and any yearnings I had to join the Air Force ended when the powers that be ordered American troops into Iraq.)

I was unsure if I would ever make it to space. But, can you imagine my delight when the SpaceX contest was announced? Then, Sir Richard Branson freaked me out with Virgin Galactic. He and those he was competing with have been hard at it in New Mexico trying to create commercial space travel.

The first commercial astronaut paid about $10 million dollars to go into space. The next few paid about $2 million each. And now? Did you know that you could do a sub-orbital flight for only $200,000??

Suffice it to say, that human ingenuity and serendipity (the Divine) had a role in all this. I guess I just need to get down to business and earn that extra $200,000, huh?! Or, I could have valuable research that would earn me a spot on a commercial space ship. Or, I could continue with the plan of being a pilot.

But, the thing I am noticing in this process is a knowledge gap. Whether I chose to ask this question:

How do I earn an extra $200,000?

Or this question,

How do I become a world-class space pilot?

I need to begin filling in the gaps. The process would be similar to our first $100,000 goal.

1. Start studying, reading at least the top 3 books in the field.
2. Start talking to those who have earned $200,000 or have flown a spaceship.
3. Write a plan on the information gathered there.
4. Make my first near-term goals.

Now, I know this isn't that specific. If we were talking about writing a book, going on the mission field, or customer service, I could write you a plan down to the minute for the next few years!

But, if I were to attempt any goal that is new territory for me (especially making significant money) that is how I would start.

LET'S LAND THIS SPACE SHIP

So, you are going to write down your goals for the next 6 - 18 months (avoiding that 12 month mark if we can help it.) We will start with just one from each category. Pick one that you feel is a key that would unlock the other goals in that category. It must make logical sense in the sequence of the others. It does not necessarily have to be the biggest or the smallest. You just need to choose the one you feel is most strategic.

1. Write them down in the spaces corresponding to their category.
2. Ensure that you are clear how they ensure the success of your Major Definite Purpose.
3. Write a plan to go along with each goal, breaking this near-term goal into smaller, short-term chunks (months, weeks, and days.)
4. Write what you are willing to give in return. You have to know what you are willing to sacrifice! (Ex. time studying, money for lunch or coffee with those people, time and money to go to a seminar about that goal, etc.)
5. Write a Date by which you believe you can have this goal complete. Keep in mind Parkinson's Law: work expands to fill the time allotted, so do not give yourself too much time!

READY?! You got this, so knock it out!

ACTIVITY: SET 1-YEAR GOALS

Character Development

The First Near-Term Goal:

_____

To accomplish this goal, I am willing to invest and give in return:

_____

_____

_____

_____

_____

My General Plan in one sentence:

_____

The Short-Term Chunks I will use (Months, weeks or days):

_____

_____

_____

_____

_____

_____

_____

What I need to accomplish each short-term chunk:

1st chunk:

_____

2nd chunk:

_____

3rd chunk:

_____

4th chunk

_____

5th chunk:

_____

6th chunk:

_____

7th chunk:

_____

8th chunk:

_____

9th chunk:

_____

10th chunk:

_____

11th chunk:

_____

12th chunk:

_____

13th chunk:

_____

14th chunk:

_____

15th chunk:

_____

16th chunk:

_____

17th chunk:

_____

18th chunk:

_____

And/Or what I need to accomplish in the:

I will accomplish this by this date:

_____

Spiritual

The First Near-Term Goal:

_____

To accomplish this goal, I am willing to invest and give in return:

_____

_____

_____

_____

_____

My General Plan in one sentence:

_____

The Short-Term Chunks I will use (Months, weeks or days):

_____

_____

_____

_____

_____

_____

_____

_____

What I need to accomplish each short-term chunk:

1st chunk:

_____

2nd chunk:

_____

3rd chunk:

_____

4th chunk

_____

5th chunk:

_____

6th chunk:

_____

7th chunk:

_____

8th chunk:

_____

9th chunk:

_____

10th chunk:

_____

11th chunk:

_____

12th chunk:

_____

13th chunk:

_____

14th chunk:

_____

15th chunk:

_____

16th chunk:

_____

17th chunk:

_____

18th chunk:

_____

And/Or what I need to accomplish in the:

I will accomplish this by this date:

_____

Mental & Emotional

The First Near-Term Goal:

_____

To accomplish this goal, I am willing to invest and give in return:

_____

_____

_____

_____

My General Plan in one sentence:

_____

The Short-Term Chunks I will use (Months, weeks or days):

_____

_____

_____

_____

_____

_____

_____

What I need to accomplish each short-term chunk:

1st chunk: 10th chunk:

_____   _____

2nd chunk: 11th chunk:

_____   _____

3rd chunk: 12th chunk:

_____   _____

4th chunk   13th chunk:

_____   _____

5th chunk: 14th chunk:

_____   _____

6th chunk: 15th chunk:

_____   _____

7th chunk: 16th chunk:

_____   _____

8th chunk: 17th chunk:

_____   _____

9th chunk: 18th chunk:

_____   _____

And/Or what I need to accomplish in the:

I will accomplish this by this date:

_____

Physical Fitness

The First Near-Term Goal:

_____

To accomplish this goal, I am willing to invest and give in return:

_____

_____

_____

_____

My General Plan in one sentence:

_____

The Short-Term Chunks I will use (Months, weeks or days):

_____

_____

_____

_____

_____

_____

_____

_____

What I need to accomplish each short-term chunk:

1st chunk:

_____

2nd chunk:

_____

3rd chunk:

_____

4th chunk

_____

5th chunk:

_____

6th chunk:

_____

7th chunk:

_____

8th chunk:

_____

9th chunk:

_____

10th chunk:

_____

11th chunk:

_____

12th chunk:

_____

13th chunk:

_____

14th chunk:

_____

15th chunk:

_____

16th chunk:

_____

17th chunk:

_____

18th chunk:

_____

And/Or what I need to accomplish in the:

I will accomplish this by this date:

_____

Passion & Lifestyle

The First Near-Term Goal:

_____

To accomplish this goal, I am willing to invest and give in return:

_____

_____

_____

_____

_____

My General Plan in one sentence:

_____

The Short-Term Chunks I will use (Months, weeks or days):

_____

_____

_____

_____

_____

_____

_____

_____

What I need to accomplish each short-term chunk:

1st chunk:

_____

2nd chunk:

_____

3rd chunk:

_____

4th chunk

_____

5th chunk:

_____

6th chunk:

_____

7th chunk:

_____

8th chunk:

_____

9th chunk:

_____

10th chunk:

_____

11th chunk:

_____

12th chunk:

_____

13th chunk:

_____

14th chunk:

_____

15th chunk:

_____

16th chunk:

_____

17th chunk:

_____

18th chunk:

_____

And/Or what I need to accomplish in the:

I will accomplish this by this date:

_____

Relational & Community

The First Near-Term Goal:

_____

To accomplish this goal, I am willing to invest and give in return:

_____

_____

_____

_____

_____

My General Plan in one sentence:

_____

The Short-Term Chunks I will use (Months, weeks or days):

_____

_____

_____

_____

_____

_____

_____

What I need to accomplish each short-term chunk:

1st chunk: 10th chunk:

_____   _____

2nd chunk: 11th chunk:

_____   _____

3rd chunk: 12th chunk:

_____   _____

4th chunk   13th chunk:

_____   _____

5th chunk: 14th chunk:

_____   _____

6th chunk: 15th chunk:

_____   _____

7th chunk: 16th chunk:

_____   _____

8th chunk: 17th chunk:

_____   _____

9th chunk: 18th chunk:

_____   _____

And/Or what I need to accomplish in the:

I will accomplish this by this date:

_____

Organization or Cause

The First Near-Term Goal:

_____

To accomplish this goal, I am willing to invest and give in return:

_____

_____

_____

_____

My General Plan in one sentence:

_____

The Short-Term Chunks I will use (Months, weeks or days):

_____

_____

_____

_____

_____

_____

_____

_____

What I need to accomplish each short-term chunk:

1st chunk:

_____

2nd chunk:

_____

3rd chunk:

_____

4th chunk

_____

5th chunk:

_____

6th chunk:

_____

7th chunk:

_____

8th chunk:

_____

9th chunk:

_____

10th chunk:

_____

11th chunk:

_____

12th chunk:

_____

13th chunk:

_____

14th chunk:

_____

15th chunk:

_____

16th chunk:

_____

17th chunk:

_____

18th chunk:

_____

And/Or what I need to accomplish in the:

I will accomplish this by this date:

_____

Adventure & Travel

The First Near-Term Goal:

_____

To accomplish this goal, I am willing to invest and give in return:

_____

_____

_____

_____

_____

My General Plan in one sentence:

_____

The Short-Term Chunks I will use (Months, weeks or days):

_____

_____

_____

_____

_____

_____

_____

What I need to accomplish each short-term chunk:

1st chunk: 10th chunk:

_____   _____

2nd chunk: 11th chunk:

_____   _____

3rd chunk: 12th chunk:

_____   _____

4th chunk   13th chunk:

_____   _____

5th chunk: 14th chunk:

_____   _____

6th chunk: 15th chunk:

_____   _____

7th chunk: 16th chunk:

_____   _____

8th chunk: 17th chunk:

_____   _____

9th chunk: 18th chunk:

_____   _____

And/Or what I need to accomplish in the:

I will accomplish this by this date:

_____

YOUR 4 WINS!

I cannot emphasize enough the importance of what you just accomplished.

Let's just look at it really quickly.

A) You broke out of the paradigm that you had to save the world in just 12 months, that broken idea that you have to accomplish everything in the chunk of a year. You are no longer bound by that emotionally or strategically.

WIN!

B) You identified your Near-Term Goals for 8 major areas of your life!

WIN x 2!

C) You also aligned the short-term goals, which you know how to succeed with already, into an organized, intentional sequence to ensure the success of your Near-Term Goals!

WIN x 3!!!

D) You have learned about Long-Term Time Perspective and have a general outline for accomplishing ANY of the other goals in your life.

QUAD WIN!!

I now dub thee an Exploded Dream Engineer.

What you have before you, if you would commit to it, would take your life farther, more intentionally, in the next year than you have in the entire last 5 years!

You have now given your dreams and desires a fighting chance. You should be pumped.

THE TRAIN KNOWS WHERE TO GO

When you set your Major Definite Purpose, you gave your train its final destination. That was a humongous start.

To get there, however, the train winds through different towns. Sometimes it goes north. Sometimes it goes south. Sometimes you visit pleasant, unexpected towns and hamlets. Sometimes you come across undesirable areas.

When you started determining the 8 Near-Term Goals above, you began determining the stops your train would make on its way to your Major Definite Purpose.

These Near-Term goals that you have before you are like determining the stops along the way. The Short-Term chunks are like placing the travelers in the cars of the train that correspond to each stop. These will be the ones that get off on the first step toward a life of fulfillment and success.

There is one more final step. It is a mental tool that you can apply to any goal anywhere at any time. You may have heard about it, but it is one of the best filters I know to obtain clarity about your goals.

For now, you have done a lot. Take a break. In the next Phase, we will really make your goals smart!

REFLECTIONS

Write down any other observations or brainstorms here:

"Wherever smart people work, doors are unlocked."

– STEVE WOZNIAK

GET SMART!

Estimated Time:	Allow 1.5+ hours
Preparation:	Needed Items: A pen or pencil. The Guide. (And probably coffee; this is a long one.)
Approach:	Review Phase 5 entirely one time first without writing anything. Return to this spot and read it line by line. Then begin the activity.
What We Will Cover:	Learn what is SMART and how it works. Refine your current 8 Near-Term goals.

WHAT IS SMART?

SMART-ing your goals will do wonders for you. Imagine you are doing a squat. Not a difficult exercise, really. You put the weight on your shoulders, and you squat.

BUT, then you get a coach to come along and tweak the movement. *"Make sure your eyes are on the horizon." "Keep the weight over your heels." "Go parallel or below-parallel to the floor."*

These modifications can super-charge your squat and get your strength up real quick.

SMART-ing your goals is the same way. SMART stands for Specific, Measurable, Attainable, Realistic, and Time-Bound.

Now, we did this a little bit in Phase 4. You made a general plan for the Long-Term Goal(s) (your Major Definite Purpose). You identified that to accomplish it you needed to succeed at several Near-Term Goals (the 8 items you identified) and broke them into small, bite-sized chunks as Short-Term goals.

You even said what you were willing to give in return (time, money, etc.), and put a date to it. That is the basics of what it is to SMART a goal. But, it is a bit more specific. Let's look at it.

To SMART something is to ask a series of questions as you approach a goal. Simply put, you ask these questions:

IS IT SPECIFIC?

This is the difference between saying *"I want to be on the mission field"* versus *"I am headed to the Dominican Republic."* Or, *"I want to be financially free"* versus *"I want to earn $2,000 a month passive income."*

One just feels more powerful than the other. It is very specific. The more specific it is the more you are able to break it down into bite-sized chunks.

IS IT MEASURABLE?

Sometimes you can be a bit more specific without being totally measurable. *"I want Arnold Schwarzenegger to know me."* Great! That's awesome. What does that mean? Is that measurable?

What if Arnold Schwarzenegger sees you across the restaurant hanging out with friends? What if he waves to you? Will you jump up and down with your friends screaming *"Arnold Schwarzenegger knows me!"*

Or do you want to spend time with Arnold? *"Arnold and I collaborate one day a week."* Now THAT is measurable. You will know whether or not you spent that one day together. You can never really know if Arnold waving across the restaurant means he knows you.

Asking, *"is it measurable"* attaches a quantity of something with it.

IS IT ATTAINABLE?

For example, saying things like *"I want to do push-ups on Mars"*, or *"I want to travel back in time and warn Haiti about the earthquake"* are not exactly attainable...for anyone.

Now, maybe Sir Richard Branson is close to doing push-ups on Mars. (Or at least a lot closer than you or I are.)

Goals that are attainable are sure to bring success because... well... we can attain them! Nothing worse than spending a lifetime trying to get to Mars for that one push-up when all of your other, attainable goals for success and happiness could have been attained here and now.

Please note, I am saying attainable, not easy. I am not saying that it needs to be something you already know you can do. Those things aren't challenging.

I am saying that it has to stretch you and be challenging, but it must also be actually feasible.

IS IT REALISTIC?

This is similar to being Attainable, but it has a nuanced difference. Attainable means feasible. Realistic is, again, not implying it is totally easy.

If you just got on your first treadmill, now is probably not the time to say *"I want to be on the Olympic Marathon team this year."*

Is it possible? Sure. You won't find us destroying anyone's dream. But is it probable? No. Is that goal the best place to start building up your faith in yourself by setting yourself up to be frustrated right out of the gate?

We can do the big dreams real soon. I encourage you to do the realistic one right now. That is setting yourself up to succeed. The big dreams and big successes are right around the corner then.

IS IT TIME-BOUND?

This is short and sweet. Is there a date to it?

Tim Ferriss put a date on when he wanted to be a Tango champion; 3 months. And he did it. If a college football quarterback said, *"I want to be national champions some day,"* he would find that he would be out of college football before that would ever happen. There is potency in saying, *"I will do this THIS MONTH"*, or, *"THIS WEEK,"* or, *"TODAY!"*

Referring again to Parkinson's Law, the more time you give yourself the more time it will take you. If you have done the other SMART steps along with all of the other Phases of the Guide, your goal should be attainable in a time frame that relates to its role.

Short-Term Goals should have a deadline in a few days, weeks or months. Near-term Goals should be done in a few months to 18 months. Long-Term Goals should have deadlines in a few years up to a decade.

This brings a sense of urgency and a constant, subconscious awareness for the goal.

YOUR 8 NEAR-TERM GOALS, BUT SMARTER

So, now that you have completed Phase 4 and have written out your mini-plans for each goal, you are going to SMART them as a filter to be completely sure this is a goal worth approaching and committing to.

After all, what we are doing through this entire system is simply trying to narrow down and identify what is worth your commitment; your time, energy, and money.

Listen to this line of questioning:

Should I commit to 100 pull-ups, or a 10 mile run?

Well, what's your goal?

My goal is to be a great long-distance runner.

Can you see how ridiculously obvious it is to see what you should do once you have established your goal?

That is all we are doing with SMART-ing your goals; refining it as to whether or not is a worthy goal to commit to.

Here we go!

ACTIVITY: BEING SMART

Simply use the table to check each near-term goal from Phase 4 to ensure that it has each element of being SMART Those that aren't, make them SMART! Those that are, celebrate over!

Use the table below to SMART the key goal in each category. If you think you will want to use this table for the rest of your top goals, be sure to make a copy of this page before writing in it.

	Specific	Measur-able	Attainable	Realistic	Time-Bound
Character					
Spiritual					
Mental					
Physical					
Passion					

Relational					
Organiza-tional					
Adventure					

oh....My....GOODNESS!!!
All goals are complete!

Pat yourself on your back!! Give someone on the street a high-five! Call your family!!

You are now in the top 1% of the world.

A recent study by Gail Matthews, PhD from the Dominican University, showed that having written goals would increase an individual's rate of completing goals by 33%! That means that you would be accomplishing 50% more on average than someone who didn't write their goals down!

The first time I completed my goals reminded me of the first CrossFit workout I performed. I was green in the face. I felt the cool tile of the bathroom floor on my cheek cooling me off. I thought I was going to puke and was hearing through a glass wind tunnel.

I woke up 5 minutes later (yes, I had apparently passed out) and felt better than I had in an entire year of workouts at the gym. I was sold.

That is how pushing through goal-setting can be. It can be grueling at times. It is not always fun. But once you come out on the other side, you will wonder how you ever survived without these principles in place.

CHUGGING ALONG

I want you to picture the Grand Central Station of your dreams and ideas. Remember how chaotic they were? Remember all the thoughts going this way and that, or wanting to make huge progress but getting the same old results?

Now, all of your dreams and ideas are loaded and seated comfortably on the train of your plan. It is warm and welcoming there. All the ideas know which stop is theirs, they know what they will enjoy when they get there, and they have decent company, other dreams and ideas like them, to chat with along the way.

You, the Grand Dream Conductor, stand back on the train platform and watch with pride. Everything you ever wanted to do, see and be in life can really happen. Those things ARE HAPPENING.

And, as the Grand Conductor, you can breathe easy now. The train is chugging and choo-chooing. It rolls forward an inch or two in preparation for this awesome journey.

But what about you? Are you going to stay on the platform?

Dreams and ideas are potent and powerful once they are written out. But they require one thing: you.

Dreams and ideas require your action, consistent, joyful and disciplined, to accomplish them.

Your friends, those wonderful dreams and ideas are waving for you to join them. You drop your pocket watch into your vest, give a glance back, and then dash to jump on!

The train of your life is moving forward, and, if you let it and work with it, will carry you forward like nothing you have experienced.

REFLECTIONS

Write down any other observations or brainstorms here:

"What separates two people most profoundly is a different sense and degree of cleanliness."

– FRIEDRICH NIETZSCHE

AN ENVIRONMENT FOR SUCCESS

Estimated Time:	Allow 24 - 36 hours
Preparation:	Needed Items: The Guide. Garbage bags. Cleaning clothes. Good music.
Approach:	Review Phase 6 entirely one time first without writing anything. Return to this spot and read it line by line. Then begin the activity.
What We Will Cover:	Organizing your world. Learn how to totally set up your environment for success.

SETTING THE STAGE

Your train of sparked ideas and plans is under way. Your subconscious mind is now looking for ways to make your dreams a reality. Your conscious mind is sparked and excited to start creating some successes.

You are ready to face the world. Most success teachers will leave you there. They will pat you on the back, reach out their hand for their paycheck, and let you go it on your own.

I cannot, in good conscience, leave you there. You see, not many people make it this far. And yet, even fewer who make it this far make it the final stretch. That is because even though their thoughts have improved and their dreams and wishes now are goals with a plan, they will still face unprecedented resistance from the outside world.

This section is to help you shape your outside world to reinforce your inside world. Your inside world is currently adorned with the trappings of the life you want to build. It has symbols and images decorating the halls of your imagination, and desire is building.

The challenge to start manifesting those goals and plans is to begin to adorn your outside world to visually and kinesthetically represent your inside world. Here is how.

ACTIVITY: UPGRADE YOUR ENVIRONMENT

CLEANING FIRST

Like it or not, the clutter of your mind is now in a round-robin cycle with the clutter in your home and digital world. There are a ton of systems to handle the digital world, but that is a never-ending funnel of information. So, we will handle your digital world later. Let's focus on your home.

Now, I am not going to spend much time teaching you how to clean your home. You know how to do this...I hope. If not, we have a whole other problem we should be discussing!

Suffice it for now to say these few things about cleaning your home:

1. **Make it a priority.** In the next 5 - 7 days, totally clean your physical home.
2. **Start with big, easy things.** Do the laundry, linens, kitchen, and bedrooms. Clean, sweep, vacuum. Clorox the bathroom. Get the place top to bottom. Just clean the thing.
3. **Organize.** Get a milk crate or large box. Toss everything into it that is in your inbox, someday-maybe projects, or floating things. This will get them out of the way for you to create an organizational system.
4. **Create a system.** With everything out of the way, make a spot for everything. If you want to eliminate stuff, put several garbage bags

by the front door to hold those things. Get bins from Ikea or make containers or compartments from upcycled wood. Whatever, create a space for everything. Do not forget to create an intentional workspace for your newfound goals. First, make some wall space for wall calendars. Second, create space for the goal itself. If you have a running goal, make space for your running shoes, your running outfit, and any gadgets for the run. If it is a writing goal (as it is with me), make that space for your typewriter or laptop. Have enough space for sticky notes, pens, creative icons, or anything that helps you write. If it is sewing, as it is for my wife, Marissa, have your table with your sewing pins, your extra thread, and any swatches.

5. **Put everything in its place.** Start pulling from your box of stuff and put it where it goes. If it is goal-oriented stuff, put it in your goal workplace. If it is clothing, neatly put it away. If it is filing, file it away. If it is receipts, place it in the receipts box. If it is garbage, eliminate it.

ELIMINATE STUFF

Now, I just have a quick note here: *be ruthless.* Toss junk away. Think Japanese simplicity. Toss everything that is a distraction or pulls you away from your goals.

Have a running goal but donuts in the kitchen? Toss it.

Have a writing goal, but is the inbox full of wild-idea mail and paperwork? File it or get rid of it.

Have a sewing goal but fantasy novels begging to be read? It goes on the Goodwill freight train.

Anything and everything that even sniffs of preventing your goal from becoming a reality should be destroyed or otherwise disposed of.

WALL CALENDARS

This is the master plan. It is the map by which we will wage war against Resistance to your goals. All other calendars will be based on this wall calendar.

Go to OfficeDepot or Staples or your local office supply store and **purchase a desk calendar**. Get the ones that sit wide across the desk that show a month at a time. Make sure there is enough room in each box and space on the side to write a few notes.

Neatly tear off each month so that they are all ready to use.

Tape them to your wall in an order that makes sense. I do mine in a 3 x 4 grid; 3 months from left to right and 4 quarters from top to bottom. That way I can see when the quarters end. (This helps with quarterly taxes and maintaining perspective on what season of the year you are experiencing. Knowing your season is critical.)

CRUCIAL: Once that wall calendar is up and taped in, take the milestones of your top goal and write them on the side note-taking space of each of the months. Break that milestone/chunk into 4 key parts, one for each week. Write out each step necessary to accomplish that week's milestone. If you are not sure of each step, research it to find out what it takes; make the calls or bring up the websites that will make it happen.

This will help you see where you should be at the end of each month, quarter, and by the end of the year. You should absolutely have a no-nonsense, tactical plan to accomplish that goal.

Meditate on this for a moment. Then, look at your other goals and, considering realistically how much you can do, add other milestones from other goals one at a time.

Pause and meditate between each one. This should be a ritual of internal commitment for you. If it goes on the calendar, you should weigh the cost and only write it if you will give it everything you have to see it succeed.

Continue until you feel you cannot possibly put more milestones on the calendar. Ask a trusted partner or someone in your mastermind to look it over critically before going any further. You need perspective at this stage.

DAY-PLANNER: AKA MOLESKINE

Assuming your trusted confidante has looked over your calendar and given you critical and encouraging feedback, and that your wall calendar represents what you are committed to devote your life to in the coming year, it is time to fill out a physical day-planner.

Along with wall calendars, you should have a physical day planner. As much as Marissa and I focus on sustainability, we typically try to find paperless ways to do everything.

However, when it comes to a day-planner and organizing our lives, we make an exception. Having a physical day-planner is a must. I do not care how much of a digital native you may be, there is something visceral and important about having a physical planner.

All the reminders in the world can be turned off. A day planner begs to be written in and used.

- Ensure it is small enough to fit in your pocket or purse.
- This is not a journal. That should be a seperate item.
- This should have space for the year to get a view at a glance of your milestones and how much you should have accomplished and what tasks you should be completing.
- It should have a week view where you can write general goals.
- It should have a day view for you to write detailed tasks and notes.

Simply put, it should be a Moleskine journal. I have used this for years. Marissa uses one. The greats throughout time have found Moleskine journals useful from Picasso to Hemingway.

I love these so much I even created a customized Spark jacket for the pocket-sized weekly Moleskine day planner.

If you do not want to use Moleskine for some reason, then you can also look to Franklin-Covey for powerful day-planners. Whatever one you choose, work with a physical day-planner. I cannot emphasize this enough. In fact, I would go so far as to say that I am leery of those who commit to projects with me and do not write them into a physical day-planner. How do I know my project will not get lost in the noise of the digital world and those things competing for attention?

Start by adding the milestones to the day planner just as they are written on the wall calendar.

Place the milestone/chunks in the day planner just the way they are on the wall calendar. Then add the week goals and the daily tasks. Your day planner should be exactly like your wall calendar.

You are now carrying in your pocket your master plan, the key to the successful accomplishment of all of your goals. But, we are not finished setting up your environment.

DREAM BOARD

All of this writing has been good. You have written and rewritten your goals multiple times. You have broken the macro goals down to monthly chunk/milestones. You have broken those down to weekly key objectives. And, finally, you have broken those down to daily tasks and actions.

Hopefully, you feel pretty empowered and feel like you know what to do with your time now to be truly successful at these goals.

The Dream Board is a powerful, emotionally-inspiring visual that represents your goals.

Since most of your goals are things that you want to happen, they are not visual yet. In fact, the world around you may visually show you how difficult it will be to achieve them.

If you have a running goal, your mirror may show you how challenging that will be! If you have a sewing goal, perhaps your early sewing designs are off-center and fraying at the edges. If you have a writing goal, perhaps the stack of blank paper shows you how much further you have to go.

This is a demon named Resistance. If we heed it, if we agree with the visuals we are seeing, we may just quit before we even get started. We need to add visuals that represent who we are becoming, to pull us onward past the doubt and frustration.

A dream board does just that. I will not belabor how to make a dream board here. Everyone who has done this has their preference. Here are a few quick pointers.

a. Get old magazines *from the library. At our local library in Lakeland, Florida, they are a quarter each.*

b. Get poster board, glue, and scissors *and cut out images and words that represent things from your goal list.*

c. Assemble it *in the most inspiring way to you.*

d. You should have a dream board for each of several categories: *Do, See, Be, and Accomplished. Each board should be things you want to do, things you want to see, things you want to be, and things you have accomplished. This last category is to progressively convince you of what you are truly capable of doing. Every time you accomplish a thing, move it to the Accomplished category. It will astound you over time!*

e. Make the process a form of meditation, *envisioning you in the pictures that you are pasting together.*

For a detailed How-To, the State of the Spark has created an info-graphic on what we think is the best way to assemble a Dream Board.

To download the full .PDF of the how-to, go here: http://stateofthes-park.com/make-a-dream-machine.

DREAM MACHINE

A Dream Machine is the final thing we will have you make to ensure that your goals are with you all the time.

A Dream Machine is a portable binder or portfolio of your goals and their plans. Here is how it works.

- *Print off a copy of your top 100, even if it is more than 100!*
- *Print off a copy of your Category goals and their milestones or chunks.*
- *Take a snapshot of your dream boards, shrink them, and put them in your portfolio.*

Add to it any quotes, affirmations, or otherwise inspiring material. Mine has letters from my wife, photos of the adventures we have had, and my Nieddu Legacy Plan (a document that projects 500 years into our future).

YOUR ENVIRONMENT OF EXCELLENCE

What you should now have is a fortress of your future. It is a comforting place that reminds you where you are going and who you were meant to be. Your home is a clean, organized, inspiring, and tactical refuge for you to retreat into for meditation and planning.

Your day-planner and Dream Machine should be with you wherever you go. Over time you may memorize it; still carry it with you. Just touching it will stimulate your mind and passion for the goals inside. Until then, read each of the above things at least twice a day. The repetition will program your mind to keep you on track.

Next you need to address people.

COMMUNITY

The blessing and curse of life is people. I won't go so far as Sartre to say that "Hell is other people." Not in the least. I believe that people are inherently good and that solutions we need to the problems we have lay in other people.

The down side to people is when we have haphazardly allowed people into our lives who come against our goals. These are often people who love you, who care about you. However, there are two human traits that most people have. First, most people are full of fear. Second, most people project their preferences on others. These two combined cause people who love you to often hold you back or cast doubt into your life.

Be wary of them. The obvious haters are there, but they are easy to ignore. It is those close to us that we need to use discernment with to ensure they are encouraging our success.

- **Join the Spark group** on Facebook; the Goals and Gratitude group. (https://www.facebook.com/groups/stateofthespark)
- **Make friends** with those who inspire and encourage you. Begin to spend more time with them. Buy them coffee or lunch. Interact with them as often as possible.
- **Create a book study** or master-mind group once you have decided who around you is truly supportive.
- **Start sowing the seed of inspiration and encouragement** in places where you do not yet see it. Your will reap a harvest. I guarantee it.
- **Let those who are close to you know what you are trying to do** and how they can help motivate and inspire you. This may in turn inspire them to set their own goals or partner with you.
- **Cut off blatant obstructors.** The time will come for you to reach out to them. That time is not when you are just sparking out on your goal journey.

YOUR DIGITAL WORLD

Now it is officially time to set up your digital world. The reason we have left it until last is that it has the potential to destroy your dreams faster than any other factor. Similarly, since we have set up your physical world to reflect the direction of your life, your digital world can greatly help your dreams.

Jim Kwik in his book *'Limitless'* covers great material on this. I highly recommend you check out his book. Though he is not anti-technology, he recognizes serious challenges with our digital worlds.

Let's start with something of direct impact; your digital calendars.

Digital Calendars (aka Google Calendar)

Since I am a raving fan of Google, my digital calendar of choice is Google Calendar. If you have another service that is fine. Any digital calendar will do.

However, I want to address something first. We have left the digital world, including digital calendars, until the end. The reason is that the digital world should serve your goals, not the other way around.

Currently, many people are using the social sphere to determine who they should be and where they should be in life. Many people get their sense of identity from this space. If you think getting your identity from the crowd at school was tough, obtaining your identity from the digital world is a nightmare. Not only does the digital world not know you (as the middle school crowd certainly did not), but there is little chance it will know you beyond the latest selfie you uploaded.

Flip the script. You tell them who you are and how they can interact with you.

1. *Set up your Google Calendar as you did your wall calendar and day-planner. Use the reminders so that you get updated when you should be doing something for your goals. Use the address function so that Google Notecards can map it for you. You should have no excuse for forgetting or not finding out where you need to be.*
2. *Make sure that you use the All Day type of event to place monthly and weekly goals on the calendar so that you can view them from the Monthly view easily.*
3. *Have a separate Google Calendar for each major project, goal, or business you are working on. This will keep things organized and help you focus on one calendar at a time.*
4. *Share each calendar with hand-selected team members. Share it with the world, but show your time as busy. That way, friends and family will get the hint that you are up to big things! Hopefully, they will begin to respect your time, too.*
5. *This should be an exact replication of the master wall calendar and day-planner. Always update them first. Then update the digital calendar.*

E-mail

Some say email is dying. Though I think digital anthropologists may be on to something, the sheer volume of emails I get daily could be evidence to the contrary.

Here is how I recommend dealing with email.

a. **Minimize your mobile notifications.** *Either remove them entirely, or trim them down to the absolute fewest notifications possible*

b. **Have a set time you check email each day,** *instead of ALL day.*

c. **Organize each piece of email** *as either, a.) gets an immediate response and immediately gets archived, or b.) gets a task in your physical inbox or on a task list that you know to check regularly, and immediately gets archived. The goal is an empty mailbox.*

d. **Labels are your best friend.** *Use them. If emails end up in the archive, I want to be able to search by project. (You can already search by person!) So, create a labels structure that makes sense for your business or projects.*

e. **Use the 'Schedule' function in Gmail** *so that, even if you type up a reply to a client or person immediately, it doesn't go out for the next 4 hours. That way others get accustomed to you not responding immediately.*

Social Networks

I love social networking. I love being able to connect with people far and wide. I also like how the social sphere is trending: it is helping people return to the local scene in a powerful way.

Despite this, the internet can get awfully busy, chaotic, and distract you from the goals at hand.

- **First, clean up your feeds** *to only show those people who are a.) part of your master-mind or projects, or b.) are the most important (immediate friends and family). Boldly hide others from your feed. Place them in a secondary feed or eliminate them altogether.*
- **Second, change your profile pictures and banner pictures** *to professionally represent you and your goals. Though you could use a pic from your dream board, I would also look for a more*

professional image to eventually replace it with. This is your public image. If you show them who you are trying to be, they will treat you as such.

- **Third, engage groups** *that are professional organizations or con-ferences that have to do with your goals. If you have a running goal, you should be on a few running groups. The same for writing or sewing. Be where the conversation is for your goals and who you want to become.*
- **Fourth, get rid of all distractions.** *On Facebook, turn off notifica-tions to any time-wasting games or apps. On mobile, turn off all notifications other than when you are tagged or when someone comments on your posts.*

A CLEAN ENVIRONMENT

At this point, your environment should be prepared to help you tackle your goals. Your mind should feel clearer!

You should have a very thorough set of goals and plans. You have prepared your home. You have prepared your community. You have taken control of your digital world.

There is nothing to stop you! There is nothing in your way.

ONE FINAL THING: MENTAL ENVIRONMENT

You have to prepare for the only thing in your way: You.

At this point, the one final dragon to slay is you. You bring a ton of baggage, doubts, fears, and bad mental scripting to the field.

I have attempted to shape this guide in a way to fully equip you and shape your world for a life of fulfillment and success.

You have everything you need to make your Top 100 a reality, yet you and I will inevitably find ways to drop the ball. In nearly 10 years of life-coaching and human service, I know this to be true.

The only remedy I know of to help others is human interaction. (Hence the emphasis on a healthy community above.) Healthy, happy, encouraging human interactions leads to a robust and helpful community. A helpful and healthy community always has the solutions to our problems.

To solve this problem for Marissa and I, in our area we shaped a community of Spark Citizens; <u>the Goals and Gratitude group on Facebook</u> (https://www.facebook.com/groups/stateofthespark). These are people who study self-development material together.

We work together. We do business together. We pursue our goals together. This has helped in ways I cannot describe. (You can learn more by joining the invite-only Facebook group here:

https://www.facebook.com/groups/stateofthespark.)

To solve or, at the very least, address that problem for you wherever you are, I have one final free gift for you. If you have come this far, you deserve it.

REFLECTIONS

Write down any other observations or brainstorms here:

"God provides the wind, but man must raise the sails."

– ST. AUGUSTINE

FREE GIFT

A FREE STRATEGY SESSION WITH ME

I am so thrilled you have completed your goals. Now what you need to do is act, act, act. Take action. **Take massive action**. Learn how to create lasting and helpful successes for yourself and those around you.

On the journey toward the life of significance, you are on the border.

You now get to set up a one-on-one strategy session with yours truly, if you want it. You may not feel like you need it!

But I want to make myself available to you. I want to hear about your dreams, how ignited they are, how excited you are, and where you are headed next!

Here is what you need to do:

1. Go to www.StateoftheSpark.com/top100 and post a comment that says "I FINISHED MY GOALS!". Add your top goal and the biggest challenge you had in the process so we can celebrate you!
2. Go to www.StateoftheSpark.com/contact and, in the section for more details, write "Top100DreamsIgnited". (everything between the quotes.)
3. Wait for a contact from us to set up your one-to-one session!

Some things to keep in mind while we set up your appointment:

Goal setting and planning is not as much about attainment as it is about becoming; becoming a goal setter and planner for life. Even more than that, it is about becoming a better you.

Depending on how many people take their goal seriously and begin setting appointments with us, this may take some time. So bear with us. We will announce it if we get too overwhelmed with requests for one-to-one sessions. Never fear, we will keep you in the loop.

If you are like many of the other people we have worked with, though, I think I can imagine you sitting there asking this one question:

So, what now?

NEXT STEPS

SO, WHAT NOW?

S o, you should now have a no-excuses, step-by-step plan in hand to accomplish your goals. More than that, you now have tools and techniques to help accomplish ANY future goal, idea, or dream.

That is the real purpose of what you have in hand: to get you off the bench, to activate and equip you to make your life happen!

So, no excuses, get on it!

Start running with this thing. Sit down and read it over and over again until it is in your head.

It is like running plays on a football field.

You look at the play in the play book:
This plan is your play book!

Then you get on the field and run it over and over.
You DO the steps you laid out for each plan daily.
You may stumble here or there.

Sometimes fear or lack of confidence or time constraints will knock you on your butt. Sometimes you don't get the time you wanted on that particular workout. Sometimes you get sick or your family needs some attention.

No problem, just don't waste any time to get back up, reset yourself, and run the play again the next day!

- Pick that phone up and make that call you've been avoiding.
- Sit down and write your first paragraph for that first book.
- Pick up the guitar and practice that song.
- Throw your sneakers on and get to the gym!
- Whatever!

Who cares if you dropped the ball yesterday?! Today is a new day. Get on it!

We believe you can achieve these things. We know you will. Keep at it. And write to us to let us know of your progress. You can also keep checking back at the website for new materials and tools to become even more effective!

Thank you for taking your life seriously. Now get on it!

3...2...1...GO!

ADDITIONAL TOOLS FOR YOUR SPARKED JOURNEY

f you have ignited your dreams and realized that you want additional support and training to accomplish more, check out these other avenues for your benefit.

COMMUNITY OF SPARKED CITIZENS

State of the Spark is a community of individuals actively seeking to live a life in a state of being sparked. They are pursuing their dreams. They are holding each other accountable. They are growing their lives. They are hopeful, helpful individuals who want to be excellent to help others be excellent.

GOALS, GRATITUDE, & SUCCESS
State of the Spark is here to help you launch!
spark

You can be a part of this awesome team by going to www.StateoftheSpark.com and submitting your email. This will automatically give you access to our invite-only Facebook group, a library of material to get you started, and an ever-growing array of free materials.

RESOURCES, BOOKS, & TOOLS
AT STATE OF THE SPARK

The following are resources and tools you can find on our website www.StateoftheSpark.com. Most of our material is free. 10% of our tools and resources are for sale. Here are just a few for you.

THE 7-DAY SPARK HOMEWORK: GOAL-SETTING

For some, launching out in downloading their *'Top 100'* can be intimidating. Perhaps you've been conditioned to stifle your own dreams, and imagining success for yourself is difficult.

'The 7-Day Spark Homework' is made to help you warm back up to dreaming about your own success. Download the free PDF on our website: 7 Day Homework. Get clarity on your dreams…in just 7 days.

Or, get the hardcopy of the bestselling goal-setting homework. $5 for the hardcopy + $3 shipping.

COACHING FOR PERSONAL DEVELOPMENT
OR SMALL BUSINESS TRAINING

You may need the accountability of a confidante. You may need a sounding board to work out your ideas. You may need a trainer who has been there and built sustainable businesses in the past.

Grant is available for the right coaching clients who are eager to grow and take the next level.

Visit GrantNieddu.com and contact the Spark Training team to learn about:

- Regular Accountability
- Small Business Systems Training
- Personal Growth Sessions
- and more!

ORGANIZATIONAL TRAINING

Your organization, your team, and your vision deserve the best training around. Whenever you want to push your mission over the edge, Spark Training (https://stateofthespark.com/spark-training) is here.

Get customized training as well as consultation before and after the training event to ensure that the systems are in place.

Some of the areas we can help you grow:

- Spark of Customer Service
- Team Development
- Vision Facilitation
- Temperament-Based Team Management
- Temperament-Based Communication

WORKSHOPS AND BOOTCAMPS

Twice a year, the State of the Spark hosts a series of powerful workshops and bootcamps. Contact us at StateoftheSpark.com to keep updated or click 'Events' on the website to learn about upcoming workshops.

Examples of the latest workshops:

DEMYSTIFYING MOTIVATIONAL MASTER

Ever wonder what the secret was that motivational speakers & gurus kept to themselves? Want to have a model to simplify and understand what these teachers are actually saying, and how to apply it in your life?

SPARK OF VISION WORKSHOP

More Clarity. More Confidence. More Action. More Results!

To go from slumped to spark, you have to get vision. Vision and Clarity together create the massive spark you need to move closer to the life of powerful significance. Vision offers inspiration. Clarity brings about the action plan necessary to obtain the dream.

SPARK OF CUSTOMER SERVICE BOOTCAMP

Increase Customer Loyalty. Improve Customer-Service Scores. Increase Bottom Line Sales.

The number 1 concern of small business owners: quality staff with a high level of buy-in. Many small business owners have worked hard to create their businesses. They simply need good employees to partner with for great customer service.

This bootcamp is designed for small business owners to invest in their employees and see rapid growth.

INTENSIVES

Need personal coaching or a spark into your small business? Our 6-hour focused intensives allow us time to get one-on-one. We extract your vision, evaluate where you are, and create a tactical strategy to create the vision.

You can build that dream. Get clarity. See the clear path. Learn how. Contact me on StateoftheSpark.com/spark-training to learn how we can work together.

ABOUT THE AUTHOR

Grant is THE Spark; a trainer that seeks to ignite lives of explosive significance in your home, in your business, and in your organization.

Author of three books, *'H.O.P.E. from Here to Haiti'*, *'Join the Fight: Go MAD and Fight Human Exploitation'*, and 'Principles in the Raw: Be. Get!'; he Sparks Vision, Ignites Success, Explodes Significance, and Radiates Purpose with his clients.

He helps emerging entrepreneurs and small-business owners to improve customer service scores, strengthen customer loyalty, and increase bottom-line sales through explosive employee buy-in.

Grant has spent the last 19 years training individuals, business-owners and non-profit organizations. He has served a variety of entrepreneurial ventures, educational institutions, and individuals determined to improve their results.

As part of his passion, he and his wife have worked in the humanitarian development field on the island of Hispaniola, in Haiti and the Dominican Republic to help rescue women from human trafficking.

They are now building State of the Spark to help individuals around the world to ignite lives of explosive significance, starting with their own.

www.ingramcontent.com/pod-product-compliance
Lightning Source LLC
Chambersburg PA
CBHW071859090426
42811CB00004B/671

* 9 7 8 0 5 7 8 8 5 9 8 4 2 *